BUILDING AN ELITE ORGANIZATION

BUILDING AN
ELITE
ORGANIZATION

THE BLUEPRINT TO
SCALING A HIGH-GROWTH,
HIGH-PROFIT BUSINESS

DON WENNER

LIONCREST
PUBLISHING

BUILDING AN ELITE ORGANIZATION
The Blueprint to Scaling a High-Growth, High-Profit Business

ISBN   978-1-5445-1751-3 *Hardcover*
        978-1-5445-1749-0 *Paperback*
        978-1-5445-1750-6 *Ebook*
        978-1-5445-1752-0 *Audiobook*

CONTENTS

FOREWORD

BY HAL ELROD

Building an Elite Organization is the most complete and actionable guide I've ever seen for entrepreneurs who want to build high-growth and high-profit businesses. From establishing a clear strategy to mastering people, operations, and acceleration, Don Wenner has created the ultimate roadmap.

Don takes the principles of personal productivity, discipline, and daily routines and applies them to growing an elite organization.

Our habits and routines create our results, and I was thrilled to see that not only does Don incorporate both on a personal level, but he does so throughout his entire organization. Don has been incredibly driven to build not only a truly "elite" organization but also to build a system that can be easily replicated by other entrepreneurs who have the drive and grit to implement a disciplined routine in order to achieve greatness.

In his book, *Building an Elite Organization: The Blueprint to*

Scaling a High-Growth, High-Profit Business, Don details the roadmap for CEOs and leaders who truly want to grow their business to that next level, <u>build a business that transcends the founder, and will leave a legacy.</u> With a culmination of the thought leadership of "business greats" like Jim Collins, John Maxwell, Sean Covey, and my own work, Don has combined all of the ingredients that have been proven to work for his company and many others into this Elite Execution System.

Key takeaways include elements such as how to develop elite world-class leadership in your organization, the importance of living your core values, understanding how to mitigate risk, how to measure productivity in your organization, and how to systematically accelerate your business to achieve all of your goals. If you read *The Miracle Morning* or any of my other books, you'll be familiar with many of the key principles of this book—from developing and implementing ROCKS, to how to leverage meetings to drive communication and results throughout your organization, to the critical importance of right people in the right seats.

When it comes to the right people or in the right seats, or what Don calls Rock Star A Players, he takes a deep and thorough dive into finding those ideal candidates: how to screen them, interview and evaluate them, onboarding, developing them into elite team members and leaders themselves, and of course, the importance of retaining these individuals who will ultimately help to drive and develop sales leads, turning them into profit.

With tools like the Elite Compass, Elite Alignment Workbook, Elite Journal, Elite Weekly Productivity Organizer, Executive IDS Summary, and more, you will be better able to install the discipline and structure needed to drive your business forward, and scale at 20, 30, 40, 50, or even 60 percent each year, year over year, all while consistently delivering wow experiences to your clients, employees, and all of your key stakeholders. Don has utilized this system to grow by over 60 percent every year for more than fourteen years and has combined all that he has learned from his experience and from others into this comprehensive guide that, if implemented, will take your business to new heights.

I am honored to be a part of Don's success and the foundation that has created this Elite Execution System.

INTRODUCTION

Being an entrepreneur is exhilarating.

The excitement that comes from change, from forming new ideas and then acting on new opportunities is like no other. Just the thought of making a dramatic impact within an organization or an industry gives an entrepreneur an adrenaline rush.

The problem, though, is that 90 percent of the businesses that these often brilliant, creative, and driven entrepreneurs start are destined to fail. And of those that do manage to make it, the vast majority chug along fighting for survival, hardly the big bang businesses their founders had envisioned.

The outside world believes the entrepreneurs who've made it enjoy exponential overnight success. Many believe these entrepreneurial CEOs live exciting lives filled with the freedom to do new things every day. They don't see the challenges these entrepreneurs face: the inability to realize steady growth, feeling held hostage by the day-to-day headaches of hiring and keeping the right people, of finding ways to consistently increase revenue, and juggling endless priorities. Contrary to the impression many have, these entrepreneurs spend their days addressing urgent matters that demand their complete attention in real time, leaving little additional time to focus on taking their ventures to the next level.

If you're like most successful business owners, you turn, from time to time, to other sharp, insightful business experts for guidance. You buy their books—you bought this one—and attend their conferences. You listen to podcasts—perhaps even our podcast, BuildingElitePodcast.com—as you try to garner knowledge, insights, and secrets. There is so much to learn and there are so many amazing successful role models to learn from that it's easy to find yourself jumping from one business guru to the next.

One expert says that if you just know how to grow your sales, you'll have mastered the key to growing a business. Another insists that if you put all your focus on better marketing, you will soar over the competition. If you follow this management strategy, you will become lean and profitable. If you follow that one, you will become agile.

Be a better leader. Hire better people. Create a better culture. Build a better brand.

Is it any wonder that people end up overwhelmed and confused? There is too much information, and there are too many people promising that if you follow their lead, you will achieve success beyond your wildest dreams.

Much of what these business gurus say is true. The problem is that if you focus on just one aspect of your business at a time, you're going to continually struggle with inconsistent results. The challenge is figuring out how to take all this advice, all these pieces to scaling your business puzzle, and put them together into a system that works.

That's where the Elite Execution System comes in. By design, the Elite Execution System provides a systematic blueprint of everything you need to become an Elite Organization. It is a holistic business operating system that offers more than philosophical advice or a list of best practices. The Elite Execution System is a detailed roadmap that you can follow—complete with turnkey tools that you can download from the Elite website, DLPElite.com—to start achieving the kind of repeatable and consistent results that will allow you to achieve all of your goals and much, much more.

MY JOURNEY TO ELITE EXECUTION

As a child growing up an hour north of Philadelphia in the Lehigh Valley region of eastern Pennsylvania, I became an entrepreneur the day my father made the decision to add chocolate Hostess doughnuts—the little black ones called donettes that come six to a pack—to my kindergarten lunch bag.

The other kids—stuck with graham crackers or apples or other less-than-appealing desserts—were envious. I came up with the idea of selling those Hostess doughnuts to my classmates for 50 cents apiece. My dad must have thought I really loved doughnuts because I began asking him to pack them for my lunch every day. Armed with a supply of mini chocolate doughnuts and no overhead or expenses (at least none to me), I was clearing a cool $3 on every pack of doughnuts. Not bad for a five-year-old in 1990.

Even though my business was short lived—the school found out what was going on, told my parents, and my supply chain disappeared—I had gotten a taste of entrepreneurship, and it set me on a path that continued throughout my childhood and beyond.

I don't know where this entrepreneurial spirit came from, but I do know that having a hardworking and loving family who raised me in the church gave me a firm foundation for success.

My mom was sixteen and my dad was seventeen when I was born. They divorced when I was very young, and I grew up dividing my time between two households. Mom ran a home-based day care, and Dad was a corrections officer at a prison. We were the type of family that shopped for clothes at garage sales and Goodwill and rarely had money for extras. Needless to say, I didn't start out in my business life with a trust fund or financial backing of any kind. In fact, I was the first member of my immediate family to go to college and the first to start a business.

Throughout middle school and most of high school, I operated a successful lawn mowing business and worked at a number of part-time jobs—sometimes several at once so I could get in more hours a week than the Pennsylvania child labor laws allowed. By the time I was a senior in high school, I was living on my own and supporting myself by waiting tables. After attending community college for a year, I was able to leverage my 4.0 GPA and strong SAT scores into an almost full ride to Drexel University.

Even with the scholarship to Drexel, I continued working full time during college, often with two jobs, waiting tables on weekends and then working at great companies such as Black-rock & McGladrey and Pullen during the week. In my third year of college, I fell into alarm system sales and eventually real estate. And that was the beginning of my real education—the one that led me to develop the Elite Execution System. I credit much of my early education on entrepreneurship to my first mentor, Nathan Robinson, who hired me into alarm sales and introduced me to real estate.

The month I received my real estate license—October 2006—was the peak of the real estate market in Lehigh Valley, and the market was saturated with agents. The joke back then was that when you got pulled over, the police would ask you for your real estate license, not your driver's license.

I knew if I was going to make it in real estate, I would have to stand out from the pack in some way. I needed a message that would draw in customers. I came up with the slogan "Your home sold in sixty-eight days guaranteed, or I'll buy it" after attending a real estate conference and studying Dan Kennedy-style marketing. This marketing message and strong value proposition turned out to be so successful that I used it for my first eleven years in the business before getting even more aggressive and changing it to "Your home sold in thirty-four days, guaranteed."

Shortly after I entered the field, the real estate market started to turn, becoming a challenging market for many. The 2008 market crash led to what was arguably the greatest recession in modern history. Although in theory it was bad timing to start a career in real estate, it was perfect timing for my innovative solution: the guaranteed sale program.

This guarantee also led me to start flipping houses—I had

many motivated home sellers contacting me, and some simply needed a quick, easy, no-hassle way to sell their home without doing repairs, dealing with showings, and so forth. In 2007, I flipped five houses, the next year fifteen houses, and by 2009, it was thirty or forty houses a year. I couldn't find enough good contractors. So I went out and started my own construction company.

By 2011, the market had bottomed out, and I saw an opportunity to build a rental portfolio. I began raising money to invest in real estate and began building a large real estate rental portfolio. Then it made sense to open a property management company to oversee it all.

By 2013, my company, DLP Real Estate Capital, owned a real estate brokerage firm, a construction company, a property management company, and a real estate investment company, together employing a hundred team members. DLP stands for Dream, Live, Prosper, and our slogan is "Passionately creating prosperity through real estate." With the help of the great DLP team, I was actively living DLP's purpose.

To scale the business even further, DLP started buying large apartment communities, as well as lending money to other real estate investors. As the company continued to grow, it made sense to form an investment fund management business to allow people to join the DLP team as passive investors.

We continued to open new lines of business and have acquired other companies as well. Today, DLP Real Estate Capital is made up of four core businesses apart of ten operating businesses in total. Today, 360 team members work across the DLP Real Estate Capital family of companies. Regardless of market conditions, the economy, or other outside forces, DLP has realized consistent growth each and every year we have been in business. DLP has been recognized as one of the *Inc.* 5000 fastest growing companies in America for eight straight years. In fact, DLP is the nation's fourth fastest growing company (and number one fastest growing real estate company) that has made the list eight consecutive years. We have grown our revenue by more than 60 percent each and every year for the past fourteen-plus years, while increasing our profit margins.

It's been almost thirty years since I sold those doughnuts to my kindergarten classmates and it's been quite a journey from then to now. I attribute much of my success to the development and implementation of the Elite Execution System I detail in this book.

IS THE ELITE EXECUTION SYSTEM FOR YOU?

I know the challenges you face. I've faced them and developed a time-tested system to overcome them. The Elite Execution System detailed in this book is for the entrepreneur who's considered successful by most people's estimation. It is for the men and women whose businesses bring in revenue of, say, between $1 million and $100 million a year, but who know that they could do a lot more—those who are driven to seek out a better way to grow and scale their business. If this sounds like you, the Elite Execution System will provide the tools and roadmap to help you achieve not only tremendous growth but also incredible profits. How can I be so sure that the Elite Execution System works? Because I have incorporated every element of it into my own enterprise, and the result has been consistent 60-plus percent growth each and every year over the last fourteen years. In addition, we have helped many for-profit and nonprofit businesses implement the Elite Execution System, and they've achieved similar incredible results.

This book is not intended for the startup entrepreneur who is getting ready to launch a new business. While there is certainly value in understanding the four quadrants of the Elite Execution System that are introduced in chapter 1, this book is not going to give you the foundation of information that you need to get your business off the ground.

I don't provide tips on how to get your first sale or how to accomplish a product launch. And this is not the book to read if you are looking for advice on how to leave your full-time job to follow your entrepreneurial dreams.

However, if you have a product or a service that the market deems valuable and that is already gaining momentum and producing significant revenue, you are in the right place. The Elite Execution System was designed for you.

THE BEST OF ALL WORLDS

If, like me, you like to read or listen to all kinds of business books, you may recognize that some of the ideas and tools that I have incorporated into the Elite Execution System are drawn from or inspired by some of the greatest business minds in the world, who I reference throughout the book.

What makes this book different, however, is that I have taken these valuable resources and—using my own business as the trial-and-error guinea pig over a period of ten-plus years—tweaked, refined, and combined the best of this mind trust into a single operating system that, regardless of the type of business you own, you can implement to drive growth. I also created the free downloadable tools referenced throughout the book, which you can access on our website at DLPElite. com.

Now, if you are ready to gain access to the system that will help you consistently and reliably scale your business month after month, quarter after quarter, year after year through multiple market cycles and expansions into new business lines, please read on.

CHAPTER ONE

THE ELITE EXECUTION SYSTEM

Do you cringe when you hear the words *discipline, structure,* and *accountability*?

If you do, you are not alone.

Entrepreneurs are strong people, many with type A personalities. They value independence and they want to be in charge. Resistance to authority—the "rules are meant to be broken" mentality—is a common characteristic.

Entrepreneurs are self-driven and passionate. They don't need somebody to tell them to work hard; they were born working hard. They don't need someone to tell them how to generate results; they were born generating results.

But after a while, the very thing that makes them initially succeed starts slowing them down. The lack of discipline and structure start taking their toll.

You probably chose to venture out on your own because you hated the idea of working in a large bureaucratic or corporate environment. And what you hated about that type of environment is how everyone is compelled to follow processes and procedures while attending endless mind-numbing meetings.

You want to spend your time out there promoting and selling and growing your business, not stuck in meetings that are inefficient at best and utterly pointless at worst.

But what if I told you that discipline is at the center of success? That the freedom to get back to the work you love actually emanates from structure, ritual, and habit? That as soon as you have a framework you can depend on to keep all the routine tasks on schedule and operational, your time opens up and your creative energy surges?

Maybe you have put yourself in a situation where you have to do everything yourself in order to get the results you want. If you have to keep your hands in everything in order to keep the wheels of your organization spinning, if you have been frustrated because nobody but you seems able to get the results you need, it all comes back to a lack of systems, structure, and discipline.

When is the last time you had the time and energy to focus on moving your business forward to the next level? How much time and mental energy are you expending on the mundane? If your answers, respectively, are "I can't remember" and "A lot," then it is time to put mechanisms in place so your team is empowered to go out there and execute. This is precisely what the Elite Execution System is designed to do.

Once you infuse proper discipline, structure, and accountability into your organization, you will find that you actually have the time, space, and energy to focus on the things you really care about. You will finally be free to move your enterprise forward.

I'm not going to sugarcoat it for you. Making this type of change takes a lot of work on the front end. But the reward—scaling your business to heights you have only dreamed about—is definitely going to be worth it.

DISCIPLINE IS NOT A FOUR-LETTER WORD

The definition of discipline is giving up what you want right now for what you really want: achievement and fulfillment. It's putting off short-term pleasures so you can achieve longer-term goals.

The discipline you need to develop to get your business moving in the right direction is no different from the discipline you would need to lose weight or get into shape. It requires long-term commitment to doing certain things and refraining from doing others.

Let's say you commit to losing twenty pounds. You have been working out and reducing your calorie intake and you are beginning to see the benefits of your discipline. You sit down at a table where somebody has left a box of fresh doughnuts. You have a decision to make. Do you give up the short-term pleasure of eating a doughnut for the long-term satisfaction of meeting your goal weight? Or do you take a doughnut now, knowing that once you step out of your healthy eating habits, it's a slippery slope to gaining back the weight.

If you are going to succeed in building an Elite Organization, you need to step away from the doughnuts. It's a matter of developing the discipline to keep your focus on what is really important. Short-term pleasures are fleeting, while making progress toward achieving your big long-term goals will provide impactful benefits to you, your family, your team, your clients, and your community.

For the Elite Execution System to work, you are going to have to make the choices that will enhance the life and performance of your business, while refraining from engaging in activities that hinder your company's growth. Let's look at how it works.

THE FOUR QUADRANTS

The Elite Execution System is comprised of four quadrants: Strategy, People, Operations, and Acceleration.

Even though the four quadrants are presented as separate parts of the whole, it is important to understand that they are not silos. They are interdependent and interrelated. You don't get one quadrant up and running and then go off and implement the next one. They are to be undertaken simultaneously, continuously, and seamlessly throughout your organization.

QUADRANT ONE: STRATEGY

Strategy, according to Jim Collins, author of one of my favorite books, *Great by Choice*, emanates from disciplined thought.

The hard truth is that it doesn't take a lot of disciplined thought to come up with great ideas. Great ideas are a dime a dozen. If you really want to grow an organization, you're going to have to say no to ideas a lot more than you are able to say yes to them.

The test of whether you are a true strategist, aka a disciplined thinker, is not whether you have great ideas. It is whether you have the discernment to select the right ideas, the ones that are ripe for and worthy of execution. It's the ability to take all the ideas, all the possibilities, all the different ways you can grow, and choose the best of the best to focus your resources around.

Designing a strategy to grow your business is a matter of being able to determine where you want to go, understanding what really drives your organization, and then executing on the great ideas that align with your values, your mission, and your purpose while accelerating your flywheel, which we will get into a bit later in the book.

Where do you want your business to be seven years from now? What do you want to have accomplished in three years' time? Precisely, what do you need to do in the coming year to move in the direction of those longer-term goals? What are the steps you will take this quarter to further your movement toward these goals? And, perhaps most importantly, how do you bring your team on board to buy into helping you achieve these objectives?

These are all the questions you will ask yourself as you create your Elite Compass, the primary strategic planning tool of the Elite Execution System. Chapter 2 is devoted to how to go about creating your own Elite Compass so you can direct your company toward consistent and sustainable growth.

QUADRANT TWO: PEOPLE

I consider the second quadrant, people, to be the most critical of the Elite Execution System.

The bottom-line truth is, you cannot possibly do everything on your own. To grow an enterprise, you need to attract, hire, develop, and retain great people. You have to be picky. These people have to fit your organization's culture, share your values, and have the skills and the will to perform the job at the level you need it performed.

In the Elite Execution System, we call these people Rock Star A Players. Exactly how to go about finding, screening, hiring, and onboarding the Rock Star A Players you need is detailed in chapter 3.

One of the hardest issues for business owners is giving up power or delegating to their team. It is also one of the most critical aspects to running a business if you want it to grow year after year. Chapter 4 is devoted to why you need to attract and develop great leaders and how to go about relinquishing some of that "my way or the highway" ownership mentality.

QUADRANT THREE: OPERATIONS

The third quadrant, operations, is all about how you are going to implement and execute on your strategy and how you are going to meet the goals that you have set for your company's growth.

In chapter 5, you will be presented with concrete strategies for recognizing, prioritizing, and addressing the real external and internal risks your business faces. This is also where the Elite Execution System's reliance on measuring operations effectiveness is introduced. Not surprisingly, the most important metric related to operations is the performance of your team members. Next, in chapter 6, I will introduce you to DLP's secret weapon: the 20-Mile March. This is the discipline of relentless execution that has driven how we go about our work every day at DLP; it is what drives our consistent results. I firmly believe that adopting the 20-Mile March execution model is what separates the most highly successful organizations in the world from all other organizations.

The rest of the operations chapters—covering a personal accountability system called Rocks (chapter 7), a team accountability system known as WIGs (Wildly Important Goals, chapter 8), how to hold productive meetings (chapter 9), and how to stay organized and aligned for maximum productivity (chapter 10)—offer tools you can begin using immediately to enhance execution.

QUADRANT FOUR: ACCELERATION

Successful acceleration, the fourth quadrant of the Elite Execution System, requires disciplined action with respect to how you create communication around your business.

Acceleration is about how you scale your revenue through a cohesive approach that involves your sales and marketing departments working together. It is about building a disciplined system to growing your brand and your thought expert positioning based on defining and communicating what your brand offers and how your products differentiate you from the competition, both internally and externally. It is about leveraging your marketing and sales efforts to scale and accelerate your business.

Chapter 11 not only covers the most important concepts that drive acceleration but also provides practical information on precisely how to leverage your marketing and sales activities to consistently fill your sales pipeline with new prospects and clients.

Finally, in chapter 12, we dive into the incredible importance of customer experience, and how each and every team member is responsible for "delivering wow."

DISCIPLINE

I understand that at this point, you might be thinking that systems, structure, and process are still not all that exciting. You might want to close the book and get back to spending time on the things you really enjoy and love about entrepreneurship. Or you may think it's a better use of your time to get back to putting out fires and dealing with the urgent issues in your business. So I am going to lay down some tough love for you, right here and right now.

If you picked up this book, it's obvious that you know that your passion alone is not going to get your business where you want it to go. You are aware that without a strategic approach to finding and keeping the right people, without consistent execution on even the best initiatives, and without a plan for continuous acceleration of your business, you are going to remain at the mercy of the next up or down market cycle as you ride the roller coaster of an undisciplined business. You will remain at the mercy of how hard *you* and maybe a small number of incredible team members can work to continue to drive the business forward. Can you work 10X as hard as you already work? Without a system, that is what 10X the revenue will require.

I am going to challenge you that it is your duty to build the systems in your organization that are going to allow you to get your company to the next level, to truly scale. I believe you have a responsibility to the team members in your organization who are working long and hard each week trying to keep up with all your crazy ideas, who offer you their loyalty and devotion, wanting nothing more in return than the opportunities that might come as you and your business succeed. You owe the customers and clients that your services or products positively impact to be here for them in five, ten, or twenty years.

Finally, you owe it to yourself to put forth the discipline, the energy, and the effort that the Elite Execution System demands of you so you can continue to maintain the kind of lifestyle you want for your family, so you can continue to make positive contributions to your community, and so you can leave behind a legacy reflective of your efforts.

CHAPTER TWO

THE ELITE COMPASS

In order to build a high-growth scalable business, you need clear ideas for where you want to take your business and concrete plans for how you are going to get it there. If you keep all those great thoughts about what you want to accomplish to yourself, all you have are dreams. If you are serious about converting your dreams into goals, you are going to have to write those thoughts down.

Studies have consistently shown that writing down your goals starts a chain reaction that culminates in achievement. The Elite Compass—a structured written tool for clearly laying out the vision, strategy, and direction for your organization—provides a vehicle for turning your dreams into goals and your goals into reality. It is the Elite Execution System's roadmap to scalability and success.

The Elite Compass Tool is available for free at DLPElite.com. Make sure you download this editable tool and, if at all possible, review it as you read through this chapter. This tool and all other tools referenced throughout the book are available as part of the proprietary technology built for companies that operate the Elite Execution System, available at DLPElite.com/Tools.

Creating your Elite Compass begins with taking a bird's-eye view of your company, capturing its values, defining its purpose, and mapping out its mission as you relate those foundational elements to your ability to attract and retain clients and customers.

After you have established this foundation, creating your Elite Compass will take a tactical turn, inviting you to create and follow a timetable for aligning objectives, assessing progress, and fulfilling goals.

I highly recommend that you do not create your compass by yourself. Take the time to do a true off-site "Compass Day" with your leadership team, however you define that in your organization today. Include the people whose values you most admire and who impact your organization the most. I also strongly recommend that everyone participating reads this book prior to your Compass Day so that everyone has the same understanding of what you will be defining together.

CAPTURE YOUR CORE VALUES

Developing an Elite Compass begins with identifying what you really value and writing it down. If you have never taken pause to define your core values, this can be a time-intensive process.

Go on any large company's website and you will see some type of generic statement that supposedly reflects their core values. They seem to follow along these lines: Treat people well. Do the right thing. Have integrity.

Although there is nothing wrong with these statements—they certainly expound good values—it's just that they are too general and do nothing to relay the actual guiding principles of these organizations.

I think it's fair to assume that every good company cares about integrity and honesty. By all means, include sentiments like these in your written core values. But I invite you to also think about what drives your decision making on a day-to-day basis.

What informs how you interact with your clients? What gives you confidence that you are doing the right thing? If you can, identify four to six of the values that might differentiate your company from everyone else and write them down.

In approaching the Elite Compass task, my executive team and I looked to the people we admire in our organization. We considered our rock star team members, the kind of people we wish we could hire ten more of, and wrote down their names. Then we listed out the characteristics of each that impress and inspire us, things such as knowledge seeking, positive outlook, enthusiastic, and gritty. This exercise, more than any other, helped us to define the core values of our company. We finally came up with eight core values. When you put the first letter of each one together, they spell out DLP ELITE. Our core values are:

→ Driven for Greatness
→ Leadership
→ Perseverance and Passion for Long-Term Goals: Grit
→ Enthusiastically Delivering Wow
→ Living Fully
→ Innovative Solutions Focused

→ Twenty-Mile March (explained in detail in chapter 6)

→ Execution and Excellence

Keep in mind that your list will likely change over time. At DLP, we take time during our annual end-of-year strategic planning sessions to determine if our list of core values is still a 100 percent reflection of who we are. A couple of years ago, we added a ninth core value: Humble Confidence. This past year, we added Stewardship. Ten core values to begin with is a lot. I would recommend sticking with anywhere from four to eight, but there is no right or wrong to how many you have. The issue is that if you have too many, they can become just your values instead of your core differentiating values, the ones that drive the type of people you hire, how you serve your clients, and how you grow your organization.

Once you come up with a list of core values that you're reasonably comfortable with, it's time to move on to defining your purpose. You can always come back to your core values as you move through completing the compass, as the process may help you to crystallize them.

DEFINE YOUR PURPOSE (YOUR WHY)

People are motivated by purpose, arguably today more than ever. Along with understanding what you do, clients and team members are interested in why you do it. People want to be inspired. They want something to get excited about. They need to feel like they are in alignment with something that serves a greater good.

This is why defining your purpose—your why—is so important. What is the impact you're looking to make on the lives of the people who work in your organization and the clients you serve? What role do you play in your community? What gets you up in the morning and drives your passion to see your business expand its impact and its reach?

These are big questions, and there are no right or wrong answers. Your answer could be that you want to make a lot of money, and that is certainly a legitimate purpose, but I've found that in most cases there is more. Along with being financially successful, there is usually something deeper that drives people to go into business and to persevere, even during the times when it's very difficult.

At DLP, our purpose is manifested in our name. Dream, Live, Prosper are three words that guide everything we do. Our purpose statement is: *Dream, live, prosper, passionately creating prosperity through real estate.* This conveys everything you need to know about why we exist, which is passionately, with intention, with energy, and with compassion, to create prosperity.

Take your time in defining your purpose statement. It took us the better part of a day to define our purpose, and we continue to update and tweak our purpose statement as we grow and evolve over the years.

MAP OUT YOUR MISSION (YOUR WHAT)

If your purpose relays the why of your business, your mission conveys the what. In other words, your mission reflects the strategies you use to achieve your purpose. Whereas a purpose is inspirational, your mission is actionable.

In crafting a mission statement for your organization, be

bold when describing what you do. For example, although DLP's purpose statement certainly inspires, it does not convey action. Our mission statement, however, does—and we don't hold back. DLP's mission is *to lead and inspire the building of wealth and prosperity with our partners through the relentless execution of innovative real estate solutions.*

We display this mission statement on our website, in our marketing materials, and in all our job ads. When people interact with a DLP team member, we want them to know and feel that we are dedicated to fulfilling our mission each and every day.

GIVING

If giving back or philanthropy is a priority to you today, I encourage you to list your Giving policy or goals. At DLP, we pledge 1 percent of our time, one-quarter percent of our net revenue, and one-quarter percent of the capital we raise. This means we expect (and allow) our team members to give 1 percent of their time (three days per year) to causes or ministries they are passionate about. We donate one-quarter percent of our net revenue to our foundation, as well as one-quarter percent of all capital we raise (the donation comes from our management fee). Our foundation is focused on creating jobs and providing affordable housing solutions. My wife, Carla, is the president of the foundation, and more than thirty team members at DLP are actively involved in the foundation as board or committee members.

IDENTIFY YOUR CORE CLIENT (YOUR WHO)

Next, in order to steer your company using the Elite Compass, you will need to identify your core client, the archetype of the person you are in business to serve. This is the person you think about when you are building your products and designing your services. This is the client you want to keep, the avatar for all the clients you want to reach. Think about your top three, five, or ten customers. What makes them your best clients? Be specific about the qualities they possess and write those qualities down. For example, DLP's core client is a principal or owner with $5 million in assets and a desire to invest in real estate.

Keep in mind that your core client doesn't have to be exactly who you are serving today. This is especially going to be the case if you have plans to grow your company and to provide higher quality or a different set of products or services in order to attract the next level of client or consumer. The idea is to define the type of person you want to revolve your business around, because knowing this person inside and out is going to dictate a lot about how you are going to go about growing your organization.

After you have clearly defined your core client, I encourage you to take it one step further and determine who your dream client is. The type of client who is hard to find or close, but if you had a few of them, it would dramatically drive your business forward. The type of client who could grow your business 10, 20, or 30 percent. As your organization gets really great at attracting, closing, and serving your core client, you will want to spend more time focusing on dream clients.

KEY LEADERS

After you know your core client, the next step is to determine who your key leaders are. These are the people who are the core of your internal organization and may be your executive team. Look also to the people in your ranks who, although they don't carry an executive title, are crucial to your present operations and to your future expansion. These are the people who right now, today, are driving results for your organization. Your success depends on them. Make a list of these people. They are your leaders.

BIG HAIRY AUDACIOUS GOAL (BHAG)

Now at this point of developing your Elite Compass, you know who you're serving, you know who your leaders are, and you've determined your values, your purpose, and your mission.

The next question you need to answer is: What's the overarching goal that you want to reach? Think about it. If you could reach just one goal that would take care of everything you needed to accomplish in your business, what would that single goal be?

In his book *Good to Great: Why Some Companies Make the Leap... and Others Don't*, Jim Collins calls this the Big Hairy Audacious Goal or BHAG (pronounced *bee-hag*), a term we've adopted in the Elite Execution System.

It's important that your BHAG inspires the ranks within your organization so they have something to rally around. You want to get the people on the front lines—everyone from the person who answers the phone to your sales staff to your lower-level managers—excited and motivated to get out of bed in the morning and get to work because they have a vital role to play in helping the company hit its BHAG.

This is the most important aspect of a BHAG—that it drives the frontline team members in your organization. A lot of companies make the mistake of defining their BHAG as something to the effect of "I want to hit $100 million in revenue" or "I want to meet these sales goals or double our profits." Although those types of goals might be really exciting to you and your executive team, they are not going to motivate everyone in the ranks.

I know this from experience.

A few years ago, we defined our BHAG as realizing two billion dollars in assets under management. Since DLP is in the business of managing real estate capital and investing in real estate, reaching the two-billion-dollar mark seemed like a really impressive goal; at the time, we were at less than $500 million. Our entire leadership team and all our partners were extremely excited about this goal because we all understood what it was going to take to get the company there.

However, we soon learned that our team members out doing maintenance and construction at our properties, our coordinators, those answering the phones at the front desk, and our leasing and sales professionals were not excited by this BHAG. To them, there was no real distinction between $2 billion or $100 million in assets under management. In their minds, neither had any relationship to the hard work they do for us each day.

Recognizing this, we changed our BHAG to providing one hundred thousand *solutions* for and from real estate. We went from focusing on our growth to focusing on how we serve our customers, something everyone can understand because it aligns with our mission.

We found a way to articulate what those solutions are in

a way that every team member can relate to. Under DLP's definition, a solution is any service we provide to our clients, our customers, our residents, and our business partners. It includes helping someone buy a home and helping one of our real estate brokers sell a home. It's providing someone with a loan to go invest in and then flip a house. It's providing someone with a comfortable, well-maintained, and safe place to live in one of our apartment communities. Providing solutions is what every one of our four hundred-plus team members can get behind because they can see how their contributions to the company impact and provide solutions. They are the ones getting us to our BHAG of providing one hundred thousand solutions.

We also make a very big deal about where we are in relation to meeting our BHAG. (We just surpassed the one-third mark: 33,333 solutions.) We refer to it in every team meeting, and we display updates in every office. People are able to start their day checking to see if we moved the needle in the direction of reaching our BHAG.

I advise you to make an equally big deal about your BHAG. List daily updates on your intranet; post your BHAG progress on your office whiteboard. Announce it in your newsletter for team members. Display your BHAG anywhere and everywhere people can see it. You'll find that your team members get excited when they see progress because they know that the work they are doing is a big part of reaching an even bigger goal.

YOUR SECRET WEAPON

Another critical aspect of developing an Elite Compass is identifying your secret weapon. This is your unique differentiator, your magic sauce, the thing that sets you apart from the competition in such a significant way that it ensures your continued growth and success.

You may think your secret weapon is found in the products you offer, but this is not necessarily the case. Even though your biggest differentiator from a product perspective could be something like having the greatest finger-licking chicken, there is always the danger that someone could come up with a chicken that makes you want to lick your fingers even more.

In my estimation, what holds most companies back from scaling their operations has nothing to do with quality of products or services. If you weren't succeeding on that front already, you would have gone out of business long ago. Instead, look for a secret weapon that bolsters your company's profitability from an internal operations standpoint, a process that will enhance your ability to execute.

As mentioned earlier, DLP's secret weapon is our adoption of the 20-Mile March, an approach to strategic discipline. In fact, the 20-Mile March is such an integral aspect of our operating system that I have incorporated it into the Elite Execution System and recommend that all Elite companies adopt it. We will talk more about the 20-Mile March in chapter 6.

STRENGTHS AND WEAKNESSES

Next, identify four to six of your company's biggest core strengths. What gives you an advantage? What are the things you do really, really well? Then take a look at your weaknesses. Identify the areas that you need to improve on, the reasons that you're not consistently getting the results you're after.

When we first did this process for DLP, we came up with our culture of high enthusiasm and positive energy as our greatest strength. Ironically, that same positive energy is also responsible for one of our greatest weaknesses—namely, setting too many top priorities.

After completing our strengths and weaknesses list, we came to understand that one of the biggest keys to success is being able to say no to a lot of very good ideas so you can execute a few great ideas. Working through the Elite Compass process helps us to recognize and compensate for our tendencies to let our enthusiasm rule our better judgment.

10X OPPORTUNITIES

The next Elite Compass exercise asks you to identify either one or perhaps a few things that, if you could execute on, would increase your revenue tenfold. What could you do to jump from being a $5-million-a-year to a $50-million-a-year company?

Sit down with your leaders and ask each other what are the things that you wish you could do but don't allow yourself to consider because you don't have the money or the people or the technology to actually do them. Your 10X Opportunities could involve penetrating a new business channel or launching a new product. Be specific and write each idea down. I guarantee you that once you go through one of these sessions and you take away your self-imposed restrictions and limiting beliefs, you are going to come up with a great list of exciting possibilities.

Share your 10X Opportunities list with everyone in your

organization, with every new hire, and with all your potential recruits. You might even consider sharing your 10X Opportunities list with your clients. This Elite Compass tool is going to prove invaluable in helping you lay the groundwork for realizing exponential growth.

BRAND PROMISES

Brand promises are the things that naturally come to mind when people think of your business, or at least the characteristics that you want to come to people's minds. Brand promises differ from overt marketing messages—the statements you make in advertising copy, on your website, and in brochures—in that they are subconscious and based on reputation. These are the things that someone immediately thinks of when they hear your company's name; subconsciously, they know what your brand means to them. Your brand promises are the things that people know they can expect when they do business with you.

At DLP, our first brand promise is efficiency and speed. Our clients know they are going to get fast results from us consistently. They know we will be able to close quickly and perform efficiently. If they need to get a deal done "under the gun," they know they can count on us.

Our second brand promise has to do with our ability to execute—our guaranteed results. When clients engage with us to sell their homes, secure a loan for them, or provide a safe rental property to live in, they will get exactly what we promise to give them. We show up every time, and we guarantee results.

Our third brand promise is to provide a "Wow!" experience.

People know that we are going to make every interaction as enjoyable as possible. This applies across all of DLP's businesses, each and every time.

I recommend that you come up with three brand promises for your company and write them down. Ideally, they will be aspects of your organization that are already familiar to clients, but it's acceptable to include aspirational statements, if necessary. Think about what your business consistently delivers (or hopes to deliver), and what people spontaneously think when they see your company logo or hear its name.

If you have multiple business lines or brands, but they share resources or work with the same client base, I highly recommend that you focus on keeping the same brand promises across all the products or businesses.

I would also encourage you to think about your tagline. What is your slogan or tagline to your business? It is certainly not a requirement to have a tagline but can be helpful to further drive your brand.

EXPERT POSITION

What is your expertise or, rather, what would you like people to consider you an expert of? This expert position should drive how you present your company, the type of content you produce, the products you provide, and your overall acceleration plan, which we will talk about in chapter 11. Another similar term for expert position is thought leadership. In order for clients and customers to keep doing business with you and especially for them to pay you top dollar, they must feel that you are the expert or the best at what it is you do.

HEDGEHOG

Jim Collins developed the Hedgehog Concept in his book *Good to Great*. He describes it as "a simple, crystalline concept that flows from deep understanding about the intersection of three circles: 1) what you are deeply passionate about, 2) what you can be the best in the world at, and 3) what best drives your economic or resource engine. Transformations from good to great come about by a series of good decisions made consistently with a Hedgehog Concept, supremely well executed, accumulating one upon another, over a long period of time." Defining your Hedgehog Concept can provide great clarity to the strategy and direction of your business.

FLYWHEEL

I am going to again quote directly from Jim Collins: "The Flywheel effect is a concept developed in the book *Good to Great*. No matter how dramatic the end result, good-to-great transformations never happen in one fell swoop. In building a great company or social sector enterprise, there is no single defining action, no grand program, no one killer innovation, no solitary lucky break, no miracle moment. Rather, the process resembles relentlessly pushing a giant, heavy flywheel, turn upon turn, building momentum until a point of breakthrough, and beyond." We will cover the concept of the flywheel in detail in chapter 11, and explore how to create your company's flywheel.

4 PILLARS

As we discussed, every great business has four quadrants: Strategy, People, Operations, and Acceleration. Similarly, each business should also have four pillars of support; think of these as four "legs" that drive revenue and growth. These pillars could be specific product lines, distribution channels, or client bases. You can define it however you choose, but I encourage you to figure out what they are. If you do not have four pillars to your business—you may have only one or two—it should be part of your strategy moving forward to develop additional pillars. A business that is overly reliant on one or even two pillars is at tremendous risk. If that client base has a change in buying preferences, if the distribution partner cuts you off or changes the rules, or if the product is no longer viable, you will be at risk of going out of business. You need four distinct pillars to ensure genuine support to your enterprise.

CURRENT AND FUTURE PRODUCTS

In this section, begin by simply listing out all of your products. If you have a large number of products, list at least your primary six to eight. Then list any future products that are in development or that you expect to roll out in the future. Keep in mind when we use the term *products*, we are talking about physical goods as well as services.

KEY REVENUE DRIVERS

What really drives results and revenue for your organization?

Which products and services that you offer are most critical to your growth, revenue, and profits?

What are the bottlenecks or current limiting factors for your growth that, if removed, would allow your revenue to skyrocket? What drives your success? Is it leads? Is it appointments? Event attendees? Speaking engagements? Referral relationships? Content you produce? Contracts executed? Contract renewals? Upsells? Is it the number of sales professionals? Is it the quality of the sales professional?

Determine the five to ten drivers that would duplicate or multiply your current results if you could only give them more focus and attention. Determine the drivers that can make your sales soar, the ones that can get you to your goals.

One of DLP's companies, DLP Lending, provides loans and lines of credit to real estate investors. A loan is a one-time transaction, but a line of credit has the potential to provide a borrower capital for many deals on many properties. So the key revenue driver in our real estate lending business is the $5 million line of credit we extend to the guy who's flipping fifty homes a year because he is going to be doing a lot of repeat loans with us. That line of credit business is where we need to focus our attention.

Revenue drivers are not always going to be products or services; they can also be internal.

KEYS TO EXECUTION

Next, you need to determine all of your Keys to Execution, which are the most important activities, improvements, and behaviors that you must accomplish and develop in order to be a healthy company that is primed for growth. Keys to Execution are all the systemic improvements—such as promoting leadership, having a frontline obsession, and driving a great customer experience—that make up the Elite Execution System and are detailed in the subsequent chapters of this book. At DLP, our Keys to Execution are building a culture of leadership and a culture of execution. They include hiring and developing A players, developing a founder's mentality, accountability, alignment, and grit.

KEY NUMBERS

Key numbers are one of the most important metrics in your organization, and determining key numbers is one of the most important aspects of achieving high growth and high profits. If you have not clearly defined what success is and how you will track it, there is no way you can achieve success.

Think of it this way: when score is being kept, people are engaged and they play or work much harder.

A great place to start in identifying your key numbers is to determine the key metrics that relate to your key revenue drivers. For instance, if a key revenue driver for your company is having enough producing sales professionals on your team, a key number for that revenue driver is going to be the number of sales professionals hired and possibly sales professional retention.

Depending on the size and complexity of your business, I recommend that you choose no more than ten key numbers. Any more than that and you're looking at too many metrics to draw any meaningful conclusions.

As your organization grows, the number of key metrics may grow and each department will have its own setup of these metrics. One great way to determine if you have the right amount of key numbers is to identify who owns each key number. This is the most critical aspect of key metrics—you cannot have shared ownership. Only one person can own a key number, and no individual team member should have more than two or three key numbers.

This is such an important point that it bears repeating: you *cannot* share a key number or any major priority. When two or more people own anything, that means no one actually owns it.

Once you define what success is and how it is measured, then it comes down to accountability and execution.

Accountability begins with determining who is accountable, but that is just the start. Next is inspecting what you expect. People respect what you inspect. The right people want you to inspect what you expect from them.

To recap, the process for key numbers is:

1. Determine what really matters the most.
2. Measure and track what matters.
3. Provide feedback and accountability on performance.

ELITE TOOLS

Next, list out your key tools that drive your results and your culture.

At DLP, our tools are primarily part of the Elite Execution System, including the Elite Alignment Workbook, Elite Executive IDS™ Summary, the Elite Journal, the Leadership Toolbox, the DLPEdge.com learning system, and the 20-Mile March Guide to Productivity. It is critical for your success and profitability that your team utilizes the key tools that help you prosper, so make them a crucial part of your compass.

EXECUTING ON YOUR VISION

The next phase of putting together your compass is going to be more on the tactical side; it is going to be setting up certain checkpoints to complete deliverables and gauge progress. I want to encourage you, however, to put this process on pause for a moment and really let what has come before sink in.

The first time you and your team go through the process of developing and defining your core values, your purpose, your mission, your core clients, and the other strategic aspects of creating a compass for your organization, you will walk away profoundly changed. I promise you.

There is something incredibly empowering about taking the time and putting in the effort to deep dive into the heart and soul of your business. Not only will it be fulfilling for everyone who participates in the process, but it will also catapult your business forward to generating significant growth and profits. If you closed this book or stopped listening to the audio now and just put what has come before into action, your business will be tremendously changed for the better.

The only way to truly verify that all of this planning and goal setting is making a difference is to provide a timetable for assessment. To complete your Elite Compass, you need to assign goals to and then assess your progress at specific time intervals: at seven years, at three years, at one year, and in ninety days.

SEVEN-YEAR CHECKPOINT

When we are creating our compass, we always keep in mind where we plan to be in seven years. We think about growth as a twenty-mile march each and every day; so, just like in a race or a big hike, a checkpoint helps you gauge your performance on your journey. This seven-year checkpoint isn't etched in stone; a longer or shorter timeframe might work just as well or maybe even better for your company. For DLP, at our pace of growth and evolution, we have found that looking out seven years gives us the right timeframe to pursue ambitious stretch goals as well as monitor whether we are making substantial progress toward meeting these goals.

Our current seven-year checkpoint will be in 2025, which we refer to as our three billions: whether we became a billion-dollar fund manager, a billion-dollar lender, and a billion-dollar investor.

We set this target over a year ago and likely will keep it as our checkpoint until it becomes clear we will achieve it, and then we will reset a new checkpoint.

Setting the goals so far out in time and aligning the different sides of our business to track that metric simultaneously creates some great collaboration between our different business lines because everyone is working toward the same internal goal. It's exciting for everyone to look ahead seven years and, as the years pass, think about how much we are moving toward reaching this big goal.

THREE-YEAR AIM

Composing your Three-Year Aim might be a bit easier to wrap your mind around.

The idea is to paint a picture of what success looks like to your company in three years. Start with listing out your top four-to-eight key numbers and determining your size/results three years from now. The indicators could include, for example, revenue or profit, having a certain number of repeat clients, a better rate of team member retention, or a certain number of team members.

We selected total or gross revenue, net revenue and productivity per person (PPP), transaction volume, and assets under management, as they are our primary indicators of how fast we are growing. I will discuss in detail how and why we use PPP to manage risk and track growth in detail in chapter 5, but for now, think of it as the metric that backs up this Three-Year Aim statement.

After you list out your top metrics, you then want to paint a precise picture of what you want your business to look like in three years. Start by listing out three big goals that you will have achieved in three years. Think of these goals as non-negotiable. That does not mean they may not change, but see them as the results you must accomplish in three years to be on track to fulfilling your purpose.

Next, describe other aspects of how you see your business in three years. What will you have accomplished? Maybe you will have expanded geographically, won certain awards, added leaders or executives, increased a certain number of clients, added partners, or acquired a new office. You could achieve a certain ranking in your industry, surpass the competition in some way, or acquire new businesses, to name just a few examples.

Use full sentences and be as detailed as you can. You want to be able to truly visualize what your company will look like three years from today.

The last time we set our Three-Year Aim, we set our sights on being the number one real estate team in the United States as reported by *The Wall Street Journal*. We also included the statement, "We are going to be one of the five thousand fastest-growing companies in America for the tenth straight year." We had been on that list for seven straight years when we wrote that statement and we wanted to make sure we continued that path over the next three.

ONE-YEAR BULL'S-EYE

Next, you set your Elite Compass to precisely what you want your business to focus on and achieve within the next year. This is my favorite part of the Elite Compass. Start the process by determining the results you are going to generate for your top four-to-eight key numbers right at the top of the Elite Compass. Then determine your annual theme for your organization—one overarching, driving message that will guide the activities and focus of the company for the whole year.

A great place to start is to look at your list of strengths and weaknesses for ideas. Two years ago, our annual theme was "28 percent increase in productivity in 2018." We focused on driving individual productivity all year long. Last year, we set an annual theme of "Marching 7,300 miles," which happens to be twenty miles per day, using the secret weapon—the 20-Mile March—that we will be talking about in chapter 5.

Next, define your top five measurable SMART (specific, measurable, achievable, realistic, and timely) goals for each of the four quadrants of the Elite Execution System: Strategy, Operations, Accelerations, and People. These goals should be stretch goals, which means they are going to be difficult to achieve. It is going to require consistent focus and execution all year long from you and your team to achieve them, but they are attainable. These are not big lofty goals that would be nice to achieve, but rather they are the commitments you are making to yourself and your team that you are going to fulfill.

Maybe you plan to finish some big projects already in progress or are going to design and launch a new website. It could be rolling out a new product or filling gaps in your executive team. Ask yourself what would be the top goals that would move your business forward this year in achieving your mission, goals that would get you closer to your Three-Year Aim, keep you on track to your Seven-Year Checkpoint, and keep you moving toward achieving your BHAG in each quadrant of your business.

Then, underneath each item that you plan to accomplish over the next year, ask yourself what kind of rock star team member you're going to need to get these jobs done. Who exactly can you count on to accomplish each One-Year Bull's-Eye? Can you also count on them to get you to your Three-Year Aim?

The number one driver to your success in meeting your one- and three-year goals is going to be great people. Decide what seats you are going to need to fill and how you are going to fill them. This will likely be a significant focus of the People Quadrant within your One-Year Bull's-Eye.

As will be explained next, once completed, you are going to share your Elite Compass with your entire staff. So take the opportunity during that reveal to let your team know that you are looking to fill certain roles. There could be a chance for a current team member to seize an opportunity to grow into a new role. One of the most fulfilling aspects of being a leader is grooming and developing talent from your ranks. And even if you can't fill the position internally, one of your trusted current staff might have a great candidate to recommend. At a minimum, you need to announce your plans to hire for a new position, so people aren't surprised later when, for example, all of a sudden you introduce your new head of marketing to your current marketing staff.

NINETY-DAY ACTIONS

After you have completed your One-Year Bull's-Eye, you will want to detail out the actions you need to be taking right now to achieve these goals. Define what success will look like in ninety days from the start of the year. By dividing goals into ninety-day increments, you give yourself an opportunity to drill further down into execution, which starts with action. It is really exciting to start every quarter with the realization that you are going to accomplish more in this one quarter than your competition will accomplish all year.

When designing the Ninety-Day Actions, the idea is to take all of the execution elements needed to reach your One-Year Bull's-Eye and break them down into more specific quarterly chunks, narrowing each down so you are sure to accomplish what is most important for that time period.

We are going to cover the quarterly action-based goal-setting tools, Rocks and milestones, in detail in chapter 7. These tools are especially crucial to keeping the company on track to achieve your One-Year Bull's-Eye. You are going to list out your company Rocks for the upcoming quarter on your Elite Compass.

After you determine the company Rocks, you are going to list out your organization's Wildly Important Goals, which we will cover in detail in chapter 8.

Next, you are going to determine the key numbers for the quarter—that is, how you will measure success for the next ninety days.

After you define your quarterly key numbers, you are going to list out your company's key meeting schedule. We will cover your meeting rhythm in chapter 9 in detail.

After determining your meeting rhythm, you are going to define your core processes, which are the most important processes within your organization, and then determine who is going to be responsible for each process.

In addition, you are going to break down your annual acceleration goals into a quarterly lead generation and expert position plan, essentially defining what you need to do this quarter to drive your acceleration and revenue goals. We will cover this in chapter 11.

Finally, list out the key technology that helps you execute each day. This may be the exact technology you have in place today, or it may include technology that you need to implement this quarter or year. If implementing new technology is needed, this should be included as a quarterly or annual priority.

ELITE STRATEGY STATEMENT

After you have fully drafted your compass, there is one additional task I recommend: creating a strategy statement.

The strategy statement, which is included as a part of the Elite Compass tool, is a written affirmation of what you are going to accomplish in the next year and beyond. It's a great way to take your Elite Compass and reduce it to a series of clear, actionable, and excitement-inducing statements.

For example, a company's strategy statement might include, "We are going to deliver on our brand promise of speed, execution, and delivering well. We will be known as the best direct real estate lender in the country. We will generate sufficient leads to achieve our revenue goals."

One of DLP's strategy statements for last year was, "We will complete the elite execution book called *Building an Elite Organization*."

Strategy statements are all about building excitement and helping to clearly communicate the direction of the organization for yourself and your team.

MAKING TIME FOR AN INTENSE PROCESS

If you're creating your Elite Compass for the first time and don't yet have a clear strategy and direction for your business, this is going to be a pretty time-intensive process. Developing the foundation of your business and getting clarity about what you really value, where you're going, why you're going there, and what your drivers are is no easy task.

If this is the first time you are seriously thinking about and writing down your core values, purpose statement, and mission statement, I recommend that you plan to spend two full days off-site with your leadership team going through this exercise. After you take that initial plunge by really carving out the time to do this well, then it becomes much easier in subsequent years, as you are focusing on tweaking and refining your compass.

At the end of each year, you will need to update your Elite Compass, restating an updated Three-Year Aim, creating a new One-Year Bull's-Eye, determining your Quarterly Actions, and making sure your core values, purpose, mission, BHAG, seven-year checkpoint, and the rest of the components of the Elite Compass are still accurately reflecting the vision and direction of the organization.

At DLP, we do our Annual Compass Direction-Setting Session in December. We do this as part of our annual off-site executive retreat. We sit down and update our vision and the direction we want our organization to take into the next year. At the end of Q1 and Q3, we conduct Compass Alignment Sessions where we engage in reflection and reevaluation, making sure we are on track with achieving our One-Year Bull's-Eye, we are aligned with our mission and purpose, and we are living our core values. This is the time we consider realignments if we are not where we need to be.

Around the midpoint of each year, we conduct our Compass

Direction Adjustment Session to see if there are any improvements or tweaks we need to be making to the direction of the organization. We do this as an off-site meeting as well. We set the next quarterly actions and also do a thorough review of the Compass and Strategy Statement, making updates or adjustments as needed. We will cover this meeting's structures in more detail in chapter 9. The full meeting rhythm and guide is available on DLPElite.com.

If, like DLP, you run several different related businesses, I recommend that you develop an overall Compass for your organization as a whole, and one for each business, but with the same Core Values, Mission, Purpose, BHAG, and seven-year checkpoint for all businesses. The rest of the Elite Compass will likely be different for each business.

SHARING THE ELITE COMPASS

After you have created your Elite Compass, you are going to present it to your entire organization.

You started with dreams and converted them into goals by actually writing them down. Now you are converting your Elite Compass from paper to reality. This is critical to the entire Elite Execution System, but it can be intimidating the first time around.

Think about it—if a year from now you look back and didn't accomplish the things you committed to under your One-Year Bull's-Eye, if you didn't live the core values you published to your team, and you didn't execute on the details of the vision you laid out, you are going to lose the buy-in of your entire team. You are going to have a very hard time getting people to apply their energies, efforts, and focus to helping you achieve your big goals.

On the other hand, if you go out there and you crush your big goals, if you accomplish most of them, and if you honor your values and purpose and mission, the buy-in you are going to have a year from now from your entire staff is going to go through the roof. That is how you build the foundation to evolve into an Elite Organization.

At DLP, we roll out our Elite Compass each year during the third week of January. We call this Vision Day, which we will cover in chapter 9. In order for your team to achieve really amazing results, they must clearly understand where the company is going, have an emotional attachment to the goals of the company, and clearly understand how they fit into these goals and how they can impact the results. Companies that do not clearly share the vision and direction of the business with everyone miss out on a tremendously powerful opportunity to drive engagement and commitment from the entire organization. According to Gallup, 71 percent of team members in America are nonactively engaged in their work. It is impossible to achieve incredible results, to scale a high-growth, high-profit business with a large percentage of your team disengaged. Sharing your Elite Compass with your entire team and having them feel directly involved with the achievement of these goals will be critical to your business's long-term success. You need the hearts and minds of your people to achieve greatness.

CHAPTER THREE

ROCK STAR A PLAYERS

In order to build an incredible organization that will withstand any market cycle, any economic challenge, and anything the competition can throw your way, you need team members whose behaviors match the core values and culture of your organization. You need team members who can perform their jobs at rock star levels. These Rock Star A Players are the key to your success.

The People Quadrant of the Elite Execution System is centered on a system for attracting, hiring, retaining, and developing Rock Star A Players who fit your culture and have the capacity to perform the job at a high level.

IMPOSSIBLE DREAM?

Finding these Rock Star A Players is next to impossible, I am often told.

Typically, leaders blame their inability to attract great team members on factors outside their control. The excuses go something like this: *My market lacks top talent. I cannot afford to hire talented people. People today just aren't motivated, especially those millennials who have no work ethic.* (That one's my favorite since, for the record, I am a member of this much-maligned generation.)

This nobody-to-hire phenomenon, it would seem, occurs in every region of the country, can be found in every market sector, and infects every type of industry.

Although it is true that competition can be tough for high-quality team members, there *are* qualified people out there with the talent, the motivation, and the ability to help you drive growth throughout your organization so you can achieve your goals. You just need to put the right amount of effort and resources toward finding and hiring them.

Most growing companies have a standard way they go about hiring. When they finally have time, they place a fairly generic ad in a couple of online job sites and get some résumés. Then they find that they cannot dedicate the resources to conduct-ing timely reviews of these résumés, and sometimes they never review them at all. If and when they do get around to reviewing the résumés and come across a candidate or two that they like, they rush through the hiring process. They talk to those candidates over the phone and maybe conduct an in-person meet and greet, lobbing a couple of softball ques-tions during the interview such as, *Are you proficient at solving problems? How do you generally get along with colleagues at work?* Predictably, they get standard answers such as, "I'm great, I am a people person, I work really hard, etc." Already sold by the résumé and their desperate need to get someone on board as soon as possible, they hire the candidate. Basically, the decision to hire the candidate was made before they even conducted the interview, assuming the candidate they interviewed followed reasonable and standard interview protocol.

I fell into this trap myself during DLP's early years, and my company paid the price for it. The amount of time and money you can spend on choosing the wrong candidate can be staggering. The statistics on this are all over the place, but a conservative estimate, based on my own experiences over dozens of wrong hires, is that you lose $50,000 to $100,000 each time a bad hire doesn't work out. Not only will you pay this person's salary for weeks, months, and sometimes years, but you end up spending your time and your team's time trying to figure out how to fix your hiring mistake, all the while suffering from the slowdown that the bad hire is causing. Then the person leaves—either voluntarily or by your invitation—and you start the whole process up again.

The repercussions of a bad hire go beyond the immediate financial and time-consuming fallout. The underwhelming performance of a wrong hire will frustrate your rock star team members, causing them to become disengaged and lose confidence in you and your organization. Hiring mistakes will adversely affect a Rock Star A Player's performance. And if that weren't bad enough, hiring the wrong person means that you lost out on hiring a rock star whose contributions would have helped you drive your desired results.

Now compare the typical company's team member acquisition practice to its customer acquisition practice.

The same company leaders who can't seem to attract the right job candidates are often experts at attracting new customers. They don't hold back when it comes to investing in client-facing websites, email marketing, online advertising, social media campaigns, direct mail, and telemarketing to garner more leads and boost sales.

What if, instead of continuing to spin your wheels making the same hiring mistakes over and over, you committed the same degree of effort to recruiting team members as you do to recruiting customers? This is precisely what the Elite Execution System's Rock Star A Player methodology advocates: using a combination of tried-and-true marketing, sales, and execution techniques to bolster your recruiting and hiring practices and, in turn, help you hire the A players you need.

I'm not going to sugarcoat it. The Elite Execution System's Rock Star A Player methods take tremendous commitment. From my own experience, however, I can assure you that taking the time—your team will spend anywhere from fifty to a few hundred hours to fill one role—is worth it. After all, you are looking at the prospect of spending forty to sixty hours a week working with this person for many years to come. I personally spend three to ten hours with each potential key hire during the evaluation process. In a typical week, I, on average, conduct between five and nine interviews, a total of seven to twenty hours of my time. That is a big commitment of time; in fact, it is the largest allocation of my time and has been well worth the incredible investment.

DEFINING THE RIGHT PERSON

The first step in filling your organization with great people is determining what your company values and what complementary qualities you are seeking in a team member.

For example, if your organization values people who are

self-starters, tend toward entrepreneurism, and have the type of curious nature that compels them to seek out their own innovative answers, you're going to want to focus on attracting doer types who thrive in an environment with less direction and more autonomy. If, on the other hand, your business is very systematic and orderly, requiring people to follow a set of detailed processes already in place, that same self-driven innovator is not going to be set up for success in your organization. You'll want to find someone who thrives in a structured environment.

Keep in mind that as your organization grows, the type of team members you will need to drive results, especially in your top leadership seats, will likely change. The doers who were able to drive results wearing twelve hats and simply getting stuff done might not thrive when you need a more specialized skill set, stronger leadership ability, and a stronger manager. When you're running a high-growth business, it is critical that you focus on hiring the type of leaders that will not only drive results today but who will be instrumental in helping you get to the next level and then be able to continue to drive results once you reach that level.

Your core values should largely define the type of people you are looking to hire. People whose behaviors match your core values are typically going to thrive in your culture and organization.

RREK: ROLE, RESPONSIBILITIES, EXPECTATIONS, AND KEY NUMBERS

How can you hire the right person when you have not clearly identified what you want that person to accomplish? The answer is, you can't.

Without knowing exactly what you need the person to do, you can't possibly make an informed hiring decision. And if, by some stroke of luck, you do hire the right person, you are setting them up for failure if you have not clearly defined what you want that team member to accomplish.

The tool to use in defining the role you are looking to fill is called the RREK Tool. RREK stands for Role, Responsibilities, Expectations, and Key Numbers.

DEFINING THE ROLE

The first step is describing the role. Sit down and write out the role of the person you need to hire, using as many descriptive terms as possible. You want to write out this person's role as if they were a superhero. You want the description to be the kind that anyone reading it would think, *Wow! This person is really cool.* Think about your clients as you write the role description and ask yourself what they would think of this new hire. What would they want this person's superpowers to be?

AT DLP, we have a position called investor success manager. You can almost tell what superpowers this person has from the title alone. It's obvious that the role is vital to the company's bottom line.

We have defined the role of the investor success manager as follows:

To develop long-term and lasting relationships with both prospective and existing investors, while also providing them with unparalleled service. This is done by collaborating with cross-divisional leaders to create and deploy initiatives to positively impact our investors and achieve our investment targets, including no losses and consistent double-digit returns.

Although creating remarkable role descriptions for established positions is important, it's even more crucial if you're hiring for a role that is new to your company. Let's say, for example, that because of your organization's rapid growth and the increasing complexities of your business engagements, it is time to hire a full-time in-house compliance manager. You've never had a compliance professional on staff before, and you are not exactly clear what you should reasonably expect from a person in that role.

Think about exactly what you want this person to do. Do you need somebody who can follow and execute on the compliance guidelines that your team has already laid out? Or do you need somebody who can create the compliance guidelines for your business from scratch? Before you can write a job description, you are going to have to research and evaluate how compliance departments are established in companies like yours and precisely what you should expect from your first-ever in-house compliance manager.

RESPONSIBILITIES

After defining the new hire's role, the next step is to determine and write down the actual activities that the person will accomplish on a daily or weekly basis. We refer to these activities as their responsibilities. When drafting this detailed list, think about how this new hire might be able to take over tasks that you or your senior people are currently fulfilling. Then add those tasks in. An ideal number of responsibilities is eight to sixteen. It is not meant to be a list of every little thing the person will do in their job but a list of the key ongoing responsibilities.

Going back to our investor success manager as an example, here is how we detail just a few of his responsibilities:

→ Delivering wow to current and prospective investors
→ Leading relationship-building efforts to garner referrals from investors
→ Manage sales pipeline via CRM, and keep up to date at all times
→ Assisting in hiring Rock Star A Players throughout the capital team
→ Overall on-time reporting, which is the accurate and timely reporting of communication throughout the investor base
→ Conduct investor review meetings
→ Assist in the management of investor events

These responsibilities outline the day-to-day activities and priorities of this role. This provides clarity to the team member, as well as to the entire team and the leader.

EXPECTATIONS

Although it is important to define a clear and detailed list of responsibilities, it is even more important to be extremely precise regarding the *expectations* or results that you need from this role. Our investor success managers know that they are expected to average one hundred points per quarter, an internal company measurement that we created to track sales production. Other outcomes they are expected to achieve include realizing a 25 percent increase in account balance per investor per year; onboarding sixty new investors from referrals each year; increasing event attendance by 10 percent per event; and conducting ten weekly investor meetings. Each of the expectations for this investor success manager is specific, measurable, attainable, relevant, and time-certain (SMART). When an investor success manager and their leader do a performance review, there is no question mark regarding whether he is achieving the desired results. We just have to look at the defined expectations for the role versus the actual performance.

KEY NUMBERS

Last, you must define the two to four key numbers for the role. These key numbers are often derived from the expectations. So, in the example of the investor success manager, the key numbers are: one hundred points per quarter; sixty referrals per year; 25 percent increase in average account size; and ten investor meetings per week. These key numbers for each team member should then be connected to the top-level key numbers of the division or organization, so there is a clear connection between each person's individual production and role with the overarching goals of the organization. This is how you create alignment, engagement, accountability, and results.

The detailed description of the investor success manager role, as well as other examples, can be found at the Elite Execution System website at DLPElite.com.

FINDING AND HIRING ROCK STAR A PLAYERS

By clearly defining the roles, responsibilities, expectations, and key numbers in detail, you will know what success looks like for each of the people you have on your team, and what success looks like for the role you are looking to fill. Once you have that level of clarity, you can begin the process of finding and hiring Rock Star A Players.

WRITING A GREAT ELITE JOB AD

One of the most effective ways to attract great people is marketing for them through job ads on job boards. There is a reason why this works for Elite companies such as DLP while other companies experience paltry results. Quite simply, Elite job ads are much better than what most companies post.

Most ads you see on the job boards are written as screening tools for the employer, rather than as marketing tools to attract great candidates. That is a fundamental difference and is the difference of being in the lead-generation versus sales prevention department. The typical job ad out there is full of "must" phrases such as, *Must have a four-year degree. Must have three years of experience. Must know a particular software system.*

These ads are all about the hiring company telling the candidate what the company wants. If you write an ad like that and expect the right people to jump out of their chairs to apply for the role, you will likely be quite disappointed.

If you are going to attract the best candidates, your job ad needs to sell the candidate on the role and your organization. You need to use the same creativity and copywriting acumen that you put into your product or services marketing messaging. Seize the opportunity to stand out from the crowd as you search for rock stars.

START WITH A GREAT JOB TITLE

Start with the job title. Think about how you can use or create unique job titles that make the role more exciting and help it stand out. We could have created another ho-hum account manager or sales professional position, but doesn't investor success manager sound more important and exciting? The job functions are probably pretty much the same, but I can guarantee you that investor success manager will draw more attention from the types of candidates we are looking for than the title "account manager" will.

COMPENSATION

In most cases, listing the compensation in the job ad is a good practice. There are certainly reasons to consider excluding the compensation, especially if the amount of compensation may not be a big driver in why someone would be interested in the job. When you know your salary isn't going to be able to match or exceed what others can offer, make the salary you are offering as exciting as possible, especially if there is opportunity for growth. For example, instead of saying, "The role has a salary of $50,000 a year," say, "Annual salary of $50,000 with a generous bonus structure."

If you are expecting the new hire to be able to earn and receive bonuses in year one, assuming they are a rock star, include that in the compensation. So, for example, if the salary is $50,000 and you expect a rock star can earn $20,000 in bonuses, say that up front with a post such as, "Total compensation potential of $70,000 plus tremendous opportunity for advancement."

MENTION LOCATION AND DETAIL BENEFITS

Next, mention the location where the new hire would work and what benefits you are offering. Even if you aren't offering traditional benefits—and I would encourage you to consider offering health insurance and a retirement plan as early as you can in your company's growth plan—be sure to stress all the things you *can* do for your team members. For example, you may be able to provide a flexible work schedule, education incentives, a generous holiday schedule, or a significant amount of vacation time. If you can offer something unusual or appealing, highlight it here.

PROVIDE A SUPERHERO'S JOB SUMMARY

The job summary, which mirrors the role description language mentioned before, is next. Remember to describe the role as if you are describing a superhero. Focus on the client whenever possible and the great results this team member will drive for the client and the organization. If, after you write the role or job summary, you are not thinking, "Man, I want that job," then you need to make it better until it is that good.

POSITION JOB REQUIREMENTS IN ACHIEVEMENT AND SUCCESS TERMS

A listing of job requirements is next. We never call these "job requirements." Instead, we get a lot more creative by listing our expectations for the candidate's experience and education under a section titled, "What You Have Already Achieved." We write this from the job candidate's perspective.

For instance, instead of saying that we want someone with a certain amount of sales experience, we'll say, "Top sales performer." We may add other achievement-oriented statements such as, "Excels in a high-growth environment" and "Proven track record in the real estate investment industry." The point is to fill this part of the ad with accomplishments top candidates will relate to.

As you draft this part of your ad, think about what background you are looking for and why. Is a four-year degree or an MBA really that important for this role? Does a great candidate actually need five or ten years of experience, or are you really seeking someone who understands the industry and can hit the ground running? Does their experience even have to be in your exact industry, or do they just need sales or operational experience? Be careful that you don't narrow your ad so much that you actually screen out viable candidates at this point of the hiring process. The goal is to attract as many interesting and potential rock star candidates as possible. You will do your screening, discussed in detail below, after you have attracted all the people who self-match their interests with the role you are offering.

TURN ROLE EXPECTATIONS INTO EXCITING ACHIEVEMENTS

Next, list out the expectations or results of the role in a way that will make sense to the candidate. We call this section "What You Will Achieve at DLP." Rather than mentioning that the investor success manager is expected to reach one hundred points per quarter—something that's meaningful only to DLP insiders—we would say, "Crush quarterly sales goals by providing tremendous value to our investors." Next, we clarify our expectations for the position in a section we call "What You Are Great At." For the investor success manager, we would say, for example:

You are great at:

→ Building trust with clients
→ Delivering amazing wow experiences
→ Consistently obtaining positive reviews from clients by delivering wow
→ Retaining clients year after year
→ Garnering referrals and repeat investments

You're looking for the people who will see this list and think, "Yes! I am great at that! Absolutely, that's my experience! Of course, I can close sales and get referrals!" It's those people's résumés you want piling up in your inbox.

INTRODUCE YOUR TEAM AND CULTURE

The next section is called, "Who You Will Work With." This allows you to tell your potential candidates about the team they would be working with so they get an initial sense of your company's culture. For instance, the investor success manager works closely with our two managing directors, our senior investor success manager, three additional investor success managers, and three investment coordinators. They will also interact with the CFO and the fund accounting team, as well as communicate daily with the CEO.

BRAG A LITTLE ABOUT YOUR ELITE ACCOMPLISHMENTS

Finally, it's time to do a little legitimate company bragging in the section we call "What You're Motivated By."

Up until this point, we have focused the entire job ad on the candidate we are looking for, not on the company. In this final section, we are going to talk about the company and why this is the best place to work, but we are going to do it in a way that is exciting and interesting to the Rock Star A Player you are looking for. Of course, you want to do this bragging in a balanced way so you attract enthusiastic candidates without turning them off with over-the-top self-congratulations. Write out what your organization values and what you do to support each team member so they are set up to succeed. Talk about your commitment to growth and how doors will continue to open for each team member as the company expands its reach.

When we draft this portion of the ad for an open DLP position, we say that we are a fast-paced work environment, that we continue to experience exponential growth, and that we are adding new team members to our family every month. We mention that our executive leadership team always works in common cause, that we operate in an environment of trust, and that we pride ourselves on effective internal communications. DLP is committed to helping team members grow both personally and professionally, and we back up this commitment by offering every team member coaching and training.

And then we list our accolades and we don't hold back. We tell candidates that *The Wall Street Journal* named DLP one of the top fifteen real estate teams in the country each of the past six years, that we've been one of the five thousand fastest growing companies in America for the past seven years, and we have been ranked a top place to work for five straight years.

FINISH WITH A CALL TO ACTION

We wrap all this up with a call to action. It goes something like this: *We are looking for rock stars to join our collaborative team. Are you driven for greatness? If so, we may be the perfect match. If you feel that you have the drive, knowledge, skills, and experience to truly be successful in this role, we would love to hear from you today.*

It's important to understand that creating job ads is a very dynamic process. We are constantly rethinking and adjusting our ads, often employing the same strategies we use when evaluating any other company marketing campaign. We do tons of split testing and other assessment techniques to see how and when we need to tweak our ads or bolster certain campaigns. We're able to tell based on the flow, volume, and quality of candidate responses if our tweaks and our process are working. From the sheer volume of applicants we receive—thousands each month—and feedback from candidates who tell us how different and interesting the job ad was, we feel confident that the Elite Execution System ad creation works. And the results speak for themselves—all you need to do is look at the quality of Rock Star A Players we have filled our own Elite Organization with.

If you want to see how DLP applies these guidelines to actual ads, you can find several examples on our website at DLPElite. com.

CANDIDATE SEARCH STRATEGIES

Now that you have written some amazing job ads, you need to get them circulating where the best candidates will see them.

There are tons of internet job boards and I recommend that you post your ad on several. The biggest job board by far is

Indeed, and believe it or not, it's free! As long as you write a great job ad, in most instances, you can count on getting an incredible response from Indeed alone. Others, such as Zip Recruiter, Monster, and your local community boards, may also be worth looking into.

Also, be sure to post your open positions prominently on your company's website and push them out through your social media accounts. For anyone who doesn't feel the need to use social media for team member acquisition, I highly recommend that you consider jumping on the social media bandwagon at least for recruiting purposes. In my experience, social media has proven invaluable in attracting great candidates.

There is a saying among marketing professionals: Seventy percent of the buying process happens before a customer ever contacts you. The same is true with job candidates. Most people don't just send in a résumé or fill out an application after seeing a job ad anymore. Instead, they do a bit of due diligence first, typically by conducting a Google search for reviews and insights, looking your organization up on LinkedIn, looking at your website, and seeing how your company fares on different social media platforms. One of the most relevant sites job seekers use and trust is Glassdoor.com, the biggest employer review site.

I encourage you to open a Glassdoor account if you don't already have one and to take the time to make your company look great. Encourage your current team members to go online and leave positive reviews. You will be surprised at what a tremendous difference it makes to a job candidate when they see positive reviews of your company on this site, especially since you are trying to attract the best talent. The candidates you want—the ones who can afford to be picky because they are at the top of their game—are going to be checking you out on social media before you ever get the chance to know their names.

As a side note, if you are doing a great job building your brand and delivering wow to your customers, this will make a major difference in driving interest in people wanting to be a part of your organization.

So far, we've talked about the Elite Execution System's methods for marketing your organization to potential job candidates. There is another dimension to recruiting that can reap even greater results, especially when it comes to filling up your executive suite, and that entails adopting some up-close-and-personal sales techniques.

USING SALES TECHNIQUES FOR RECRUITING

Sometimes, especially when filling senior roles, you need to treat recruiting as if it were any other form of business development, starting in your own sphere of influence. Look through your Rolodex, at your customer relationship management (CRM) system, and at your LinkedIn contacts. Think about the people you encounter during your workday, people who work with competitors, even people who might *be* your competitors. Think about your vendors, your clients, anyone who has crossed your path who made you think, "Man, if I had this person in our organization, they'd be a rock star."

One of your best talent recruitment resources is your current workforce. Make sure they know that you're hiring so they can spread the word. Don't just depend on HR to do the recruiting. Instead, make recruiting part of your company culture, something that everyone participates in.

Approach your rock stars and ask them for referrals. Great producers recognize other great producers. If you have people in your organization who've worked for your competitors, they'll probably be able to identify people at their former companies who could be a good fit at your organization. Talk to them and see if they're still in touch with old colleagues.

Another way to attract great people is through industry engagement. Attend events, and talk to people. When I go to industry events, I'm as focused on connecting with people I can hire as I am looking for new clients or new business.

I admit it—I love recruiting new team members from my competitors, and I recommend that, whenever possible, you do the same. Not only do your best competitors often have great people who already know your industry and clients, but they also know the tactics of those competitors and can bring that knowledge to you. And an added bonus is that if you recruit the top rock stars from your competitors, it will often set them back as well. I have done this at all levels, from senior executives to frontline property managers, and it has given us many of our very best rock star team members.

For example, when we buy an apartment community that typically is underperforming at the time of our purchase, one of the first things we do is hire a rock star property manager to lead the community. We always know the top competitors who have the highest occupancies and the best reputations in the area. Who better to recruit to drive results at our recently purchased community than the manager driving results at the community down the street? This is someone who has already done what we need to do, who understands the market, and has relationships with the best residents, potential team members, and vendors. People often move to a community or leave a community over their relationship with the manager. We have recruited many of our best managers directly from our competition.

Another great example is sales. When I need to hire a great sales producer or manager, either I or someone in my company will pick up the phone and call the sales manager or top rep at our best competitor. Not only does this person already know our industry, but they can also bring along their existing clients and even be an inside source for hiring additional producers from the competitor.

You also might want to consider utilizing the services of a recruiter, but only in addition to—never as a total replacement for—you and your senior leaders focusing on recruiting great people yourselves. Depending on the size of your organization and the pace of growth, you might consider bringing on an in-house recruiter. An external recruiter will typically charge between 25 and 35 percent of the year one compensation for a new recruit. Both internal and external recruiters are a hefty cost, but the reward of bringing the rock star team member you need on board can be worth the investment.

If you consider going with an external recruiter, I recommend taking the time to really interview the recruiting firm and ask for references. We have used an external recruiter to fill eight to ten key leadership seats and a few sales seats over the past few years, and they have brought us some of our very best leaders, making it well worth the cost.

SCREENING AND EVALUATING CANDIDATES

Before my company adopted strong candidate screening methods, I would meet with every candidate whose résumé looked promising. Even though I knew within a few minutes if the candidate was not going to be a fit for DLP, I was too nice to just tell them that right away. I would waste half an hour or more of both our time having a conversation with somebody who I was never going to hire just so I wouldn't make the person feel bad. What's even worse is I was not, in reality, being a nice guy. All I was doing was giving the candidate false hope. Interviewing prospective team members without thoroughly screening them wasn't fair to anyone.

Failing to properly screen candidates is always a losing practice. Either you end up wasting everyone's time like I used to do or you end up forgoing the interview process altogether. Both scenarios lead to the same place, with you failing to fill seats with rock stars.

ELITE CANDIDATE SCREENING TOOLS

The screening tools I am introducing here can help you more closely identify likely matches and minimize the time spent interviewing the candidates who are not going to be the rock stars you need. Here is our protocol.

Once we identify a candidate that we are interested in evaluating for a role at DLP, we email and call the candidates we are interested in using the script and template found on the

DLP website (see DLPElite.com). We let them know we are interested in evaluating them for a role and need them to complete a few steps, including a video interview and two short predictive index assessments.

For the video interview, we ask candidates to record answers to ten questions via video, using Spark Hire technology (sparkhire.com). We have a different DLP team member ask each of these pre-recorded questions via video so the candidate gets a personal feeling for our company by being introduced to some members of our team, at least through a video recording.

We are thoughtful about the questions we ask. Many are around personality and behavior. We are continually tweaking and evaluating these questions. For instance, we might ask, *What characteristics do you think the most successful people in the world have?* or *What's the last great business book you read and why?*

We aren't just interested in what they did in their last job or how they rate their leadership abilities. We are looking for answers that will help us get a better understanding of who the person is and whether they would be a good culture fit for our organization.

Our last question is always, *What is your ideal compensation?* We purposefully don't ask what specific salary they require. Although some people skirt the answer regardless, most give us an idea if we are a likely fit from a compensation standpoint.

The video interview takes from ten to thirty minutes for a candidate to complete. Once completed, the candidate moves on to the second step in the process by clicking on a link to our Predictive Index (PI) system. Each candidate is asked to complete two PI assessments. The first is a five-minute behavioral assessment that helps us assess if their behaviors are a match for our culture and the needs of this role, and the second is a twelve-minute cognitive assessment that basically gauges their processing speed.

We put a lot of time and effort on the front end of these assessments. As soon as we decide we are going to hire for a position, the people responsible for filling that role complete a job profile in the PI system. That way, we can see if the results of the candidate's behavioral assessment match up with what we are looking for. We don't just get raw results; we get a comparison of how the results line up with our predetermined criteria.

With respect to the cognitive assessment, we preset a target cognitive score that makes sense for the role in question. Cognitive assessments are actually the number one determining factor for job success, especially for anyone being hired in a high-growth environment. You need someone who can jump on board and get up to speed as quickly as possible. This tool is essential in making sure you find people to help you scale your business quickly.

The whole process—from the Spark Hire video recorded interview to PI—takes the candidate less than an hour. Results are emailed immediately to the relevant leaders involved in the screening and hiring of the role, who then determine whether to schedule an interview or pass on the candidate.

ELITE CANDIDATE INTERVIEW PROCESS

We have adopted and modified the job candidate interviewing

process developed by Brad Smart called Topgrading, which is outlined in his 2005 book, *Topgrading (How to Hire, Coach and Keep A Players)*.

We typically start with an introductory video interview over Zoom, usually conducted by one leader who is heavily involved with the role—which may be the direct reporting manager, the business unit leader, or, at times, me. This interview is really a "get to know you" interaction to determine if the candidate would be a cultural fit and to start diving into the weeds on their experience in order to get a feel for whether they have the experience to do the job at a high level.

If that interview goes well, we invite the candidate to come to our offices and participate in a panel interview. If the candidate is not local, we may do the panel interview via Zoom.

Unlike the initial interview, this panel conducts a very deep elite topgrading interview where we push hard, getting into uncomfortable questions as we walk the candidate through each step in their career history. Our intention is to get them beyond the interview face that they're used to putting on and, instead, get to the real person. The panel interview is a big time investment—it can easily last three hours—but that is what it takes to dig deep.

If we have done our job right up to this point—writing great job ads, using the screening tools, really evaluating the video interview and the assessments, and then utilizing the introductory interview effectively—we usually end up with somewhere between 30 and 70 percent of the candidates who make it to the panel interview turning out to be a rock star we want to hire.

After the panel interview, you need to make sure you take time to huddle with the people involved and fully flesh out everyone's feedback on the candidate. At DLP, we keep a Google Drive folder for each candidate with a copy of their video interview, the results of their assessments, their résumé, and all the notes and comments from each team member involved in the interview process.

It is important to make sure you receive feedback from all stakeholders in the potential hire. You will not have 100 percent buy-in from everyone on each candidate you decide to make an offer to, but you want to make sure you obtain everyone's feedback and fully flesh out any and all concerns.

If we decide after the panel interview that we are likely to make an offer to the candidate, we usually engage in at least one final interview, typically with the final decision maker, to flesh out any last questions or concerns. If the panel interview was done via Zoom, it is important for this final interview to be conducted face-to-face. Do not ever hire a candidate without spending face-to-face time.

I often do this final interview via a walk and talk, where I get the candidate out of the office and take them for a walk. I have found the walk and talk to be incredibly powerful for interviewing candidates, as well as for coaching and gaining alignment with my reports, and have even used it for sales meetings.

Depending on the role, we may also have the candidate go into the field with the team for a day, join some of our existing meetings, or find other ways to get them to spend time outside of the normal interview process.

In addition, throughout the process, we provide candidates with job-specific assessments that they must complete. If we are hiring an analyst or underwriter, we will give them a deal to underwrite. If we are hiring someone in marketing, we give them a marketing assignment. For a property manager, we have them shop a community and give us a report on what they see, what should change, and so forth.

Last, it is very important to obtain references and actually follow through on a conversation with them. This lets you deep dive into any potential concerns about the candidate via questions that will shed light on areas of hesitation.

I know that what I am describing is an enormous process in terms of time and resources, especially considering that we, ideally, are engaged in this process with a few candidates simultaneously for the same position. I promise you, however, that the resources you dedicate to finding and hiring Rock Star A Players will reap tremendous results. Spending the time and resources to assess, interview, and hire Rock Star A Players is the only way to grow an Elite Organization. You simply cannot have an Elite Organization without the very best.

REMEMBER, YOU ARE BEING EVALUATED, TOO

Keep in mind that throughout this whole process, you and your company are being interviewed and evaluated as well. The candidates are going to be making a lot of assumptions based on how professional you were through that interview process, how insightful the questions were, and how the follow-up process went.

Throughout the interview process, you need to be gauging

the candidate's interest. We make it a point to ask questions designed to identify any concerns they might have about working with our company such as, *Are there any hesitations you'd have in accepting this job? What do you think would be the biggest challenge that you would have in being able to perform at a high level in this role? Do you expect that you'd accept a job offer if we moved forward with one?*

There's nothing more frustrating than investing all this time, getting all the way to the point that you decide a person is a perfect fit, making an offer, and then being rejected because the candidate decides to either go with another opportunity or to stay with the company they work for now. The best people will often be evaluating multiple roles at the same time, and you need to make sure you are asking the right questions so you are aware of what the candidate is looking for in their next opportunity and company. Also, make sure you ask them if they are actively evaluating other opportunities. If they are, do not hesitate to ask for details—what types of roles, what do they like about that opportunity, how does it compare to this opportunity, what would cause them to take that opportunity instead. Ask them what stage they are in that process and the expected time table. You do not want to find out that they have an offer on the table now and that you will need to accelerate the timing of your interview process. Do not hesitate to ask specifically whom they are interviewing with as well.

MAKING A CAREER SUCCESS OFFER

The last important step in hiring a great person is presenting them with a job offer that's attractive enough to accept. Rather than calling it a job offer, we say that we are presenting a career success offer. Just like the job description, we write the career success offer in a way that is unique and attractive.

Do not just email the offer over or delegate this task to HR. Instead, make a point to deliver the offer in a face-to-face format, even if that means using video conferencing as a last resort. Either you or one of your top leaders should deliver the job offer personally, with excitement and energy. You want to show the candidate how happy you are about bringing them on board, while at the same time emphasizing the great opportunity that you are offering them.

Prepare in advance for any questions or concerns that could arise when you make your offer. You want to be able to overcome objections right away, using your responses to get them excited about the role. For example, if you know the candidate wants an annual salary of $100,000, but you can offer them only $70,000, be prepared to emphasize the potential for their compensation to increase substantially as the company grows. Use this conversation as a way to highlight the great opportunity that you are offering them.

ONBOARDING NEW ROCK STARS

Once you successfully hire a Rock Star A player, it's important to make sure they experience a great onboarding process where, again, you make it extremely clear what you want from that person and what the desired outcomes are. Your goal is to set them up for success.

High-growth companies are notorious for hiring great candidates and then leaving them on their own to figure out what they need to do. Without an organized onboarding process—especially if it's a new role that doesn't yet exist in the organization—the lack of direction and access to information can set the new hire up for failure.

DLP is a high-growth company, and even though we have tried to put systems in place to onboard a new team member, we know that we aren't perfect. We make it a point to tell every person who comes aboard, *Look, we know what your first couple of weeks are going to be like. We're an organization with a lot of fast-moving pieces and it can be overwhelming. You're going to feel like you're drinking from a fire hose at times, and that's okay; that's to be expected.*

Although you don't need to have an incredibly detailed six-month onboarding process like they do in *Fortune* 500 companies, you owe it to your new hires to have some sort of structure. At DLP, we set up lots of little touch points to not only familiarize the new hires with our systems and procedures but also to help them feel a connection with the organization. Right away, we want them to understand their value. The following are some of the ways we do this:

→ We send each new team member a welcome package prior to their start date. This package typically contains an assortment of company gear; either this book, *Building an Elite Organization* (for senior leaders), or the team member guide, Driven for Greatness: *Thriving in an Elite Organization* (for frontline team members); the Elite Journal; and a padfolio.
→ We provide access to all of our Elite Tools prior to their start date.
→ We provide a culture guide—our alternative to the typical team member handbook—that includes the history of our

organization, our company values, and additional useful insights into our company culture.

→ We issue each person a customized onboarding workbook that clearly outlines their entire first two weeks on the job, including what trainings to watch first on our online training system, what one-on-one meetings to schedule, important information they will need to learn, and the ongoing meetings they will be expected to join.

→ We provide a complete schedule for their first day, which includes:

» An introduction to the whole company via our morning huddle

» Cultural onboarding with our rock star acceleration manager (a full-time team member focused on onboarding and developing team members)

» An IT setup meeting covering all of our systems and technology

» A group welcome call between all day-one team members and our chief of staff

» A call with their buddy (explained below)

→ We provide them with a thirty-day 20-Mile March checklist (see chapter 6) to make sure they receive access to and training on everything they need to be set up for success.

→ For new hires not working from our headquarters, we arrange a trip to visit the DLP home offices within their first two weeks of employment.

→ We hold a monthly Welcome to DLP meeting in which I personally tell the new hire our story and explain our culture, our compass, how they fit into our vision, and answer any and all questions.

→ We send an email out to all team members announcing our new hire, providing the person's photo and background, and letting everyone know what their role and responsibilities are so they can shoot back welcome notes and well wishes.

→ We do a formal introduction of the new team member via a company-wide Monday morning Zoom huddle with the whole company.

As mentioned previously, each new DLP team member is introduced to a buddy on their first day. This is somebody who knows the organization well and is a great cultural leader. This person does not have to be in the same type of position or even at the same hierarchical level. We've paired executives with maintenance engineers, and we've seen great friendships develop between buddies. We look for established team members who walk the Elite Execution System walk and who can help new hires fit into DLP's culture.

All new team members have access to our training system, DLP Edge, the online tool referred to in their onboarding materials. DLP Edge is a tool that they will access and use throughout their career with us. It contains a library of recorded and interactive trainings, tests, and assessments to help team members grow, learn, and sharpen their skills. Because we bombard new hires with a lot of information and personal attention the first couple of weeks, by the end of the second week, they are already in a rhythm with the company and they don't feel new anymore. By the third week or so, we start to expect them to have a decent level of output as we continue to onboard them and infuse them into our culture. I have found that taking this time to create a high level of engagement in the first few weeks of employment, even if it interferes with immediate productivity, makes a dramatic difference in the long term and, as importantly, in our ability to retain new hires as valued team members.

DEVELOPMENT AND RETENTION

Every valued team member deserves a path to development. Rock stars don't want to be stagnant; they want to develop personally and professionally. It's up to you as the company's leader to make sure that your organization provides opportunities for each individual to grow. That is key to their ongoing engagement, longevity, and ability to continue to remain A players and drive tremendous results in helping your company grow.

In order to develop your people, you must really care about each of them as a person. You must care about their success. I know that sounds simple and maybe cliché, but it is critical that you truly care and, as importantly, that you show them you are willing to invest in them. This means you need to show an interest in more than your team members' job performance.

In addition, it is important to support people in achieving their career goals. If a particular team member wants to evolve from their role as a frontline producer into an executive leader, for example, you need to provide them with a clear path to get there, complete with how they will be held accountable for their own upwardly mobile journey.

At DLP, we want our team members to achieve success in all areas of their lives, including their home lives and their spiritual lives. This is one of our core values: Living Fully. When your team members see that you're invested in them as people, they're going to be willing to go through walls for you. They're going to feel committed to you. They're not going to jump every time a recruiter calls or every time another opportunity comes along where they can make a little bit more money.

Later, I will be introducing our Elite Alignment tool and explaining how we conduct alignment meetings. Both allow leadership to better understand our team members and give them real feedback, coaching, and accountability. Also, in the Elite Alignment Workbook is a development plan that will help our team members to execute in their current role, as well as advance to the desired next step in their career. Focusing on alignment helps us to understand each team member's aspirations and goals—both short term and long term—so we can work with them on an ongoing development plan to achieve their goals and have the feeling of fulfillment that we all want.

CHAPTER FOUR

ELITE WORLD-CLASS LEADERSHIP

If you want to truly achieve consistent long-term scalability, *you* must find and develop great leaders within your organization. You must live the motto that we use at DLP, one that I encourage you to adopt: *Leaders made here.*

In order to become an Elite World-Class Leader, you must provide your rock stars with the opportunity, authority, and accountability to lead.

EMPOWERMENT

Giving up even a portion of control over a company you created or grew and nurtured can be very difficult. If you are like most entrepreneurs, you are used to taking charge. Deferring judgment to others may seem counterintuitive. An entrepreneur by nature grabs hold of a project, dives into an issue, and drives solutions forward. This can-do spirit is how successful people like you get a new enterprise off the ground, and it is how you got to the point where scaling your business is happening or is actually within reach.

However, if every major decision starts and stops with you, if nothing can get done without your direction, if you're doing all the important work yourself, you are going to struggle to move your business forward and truly scale. If you can't or won't empower individuals within your organization to make unilateral decisions, to lead team members without your direct supervision, and to contribute in meaningful ways to the future of your enterprise, then you will never be able to realize exponential growth. You simply cannot do it all.

I am not suggesting that you turn some aspects of your operations over to others on blind faith. Quite the contrary. I am suggesting that you first become an Elite World-Class Leader and then develop other leaders whom you can count on.

To build a truly enduring organization, you must go from being a time teller to a clock builder. This means you must go from everyone needing to come to you for every decision to instead building an organization full of people who are empowered and have the ability to make decisions.

Jim Collins explains this best in an article he published many years ago:

"Imagine that you met a remarkable person who could look at the sun or the stars and, amazingly, state the exact time and date. Wouldn't it be even more amazing still if, instead of telling the time, that person built a clock that could tell the time forever, even after he or she were dead and gone?"

"Having a great idea or being a charismatic visionary leader is 'time telling'; building a company that can prosper far beyond the tenure of any single leader and through multiple product life cycles is 'clock building.' Those who build visionary companies tend to be clock builders. Their primary accomplishment is not the implementation of a great idea, the expression of a charismatic personality, or the accumulation of wealth. It is the company itself and what it stands for."

DEFINE WHAT LEADERSHIP MEANS IN YOUR COMPANY

In order to attract, nurture, and support world-class leaders, it is critical that you take the time to define what leadership means for your company.

In his book *Leaders Made Here: Building a Leadership Culture*, vice president of high performance leadership at Chick-fil-A Inc. and best-selling author Mark Miller points out that there is real power in forging a common definition of leadership. In fact, Miller says that taking the time to create a definition of leadership as it pertains to your company is the first step in creating a culture of leadership.

I've spent a tremendous amount of time studying how great business leaders define leadership and have always been particularly drawn to author and the forefather of leadership, John Maxwell. Maxwell defines leadership simply as "leadership is influence."

After careful thought, we've developed our own definition of leadership that expands on Maxwell's, qualifying the type of leaders we aspire to be while also incorporating DLP's results-driven culture. The DLP definition has evolved to be:

> Leadership is defined by results. It is the capacity to influence others through inspiration and passion, generated by vision, ignited by a purpose, and produced by conviction.

Many of the current and future leaders in my company know this definition by heart. They understand that it is designed to inform their day-to-day behaviors and attitudes. As you work to create your own definition of leadership, you may want to use this definition as inspiration, the way I used John Maxwell's; or, if it really resonates with you, feel free to borrow the DLP definition in whole or in part.

JOB OF A LEADER

After you define what leadership is in your organization, I recommend you define the job of a leader. Here is our definition of the job of a leader, which you again are welcome to copy in part or in full.

The job of a leader is very simple: "Leaders make things easy so that the team can execute. Leaders show the way through the forest in order for the team to achieve its goals by teaching, coaching, and empowering."

To elaborate a bit further on what leaders do:

Leaders make things easier by taking control and removing pressure from everyone else. They identify, discuss, and solve problems; they allow decisions to be made.

This requires critical thinking. Leadership is the ability to see the whole picture, or at least enough of it to be able to see the root of a problem, and then build solutions.

Leaders make things easier by being able to simplify the complex.

Leaders are able to solve problems largely because they have influence; and people are willing and want to follow their direction. People trust the leader's decision-making abilities.

LEVEL 5 LEADERSHIP: SERVANT LEADERSHIP

The concept of Level 5 Leadership is based on John Maxwell's *The 5 Levels of Leadership* (one of the best books on leadership ever written) and Jim Collins's *Good to Great* (one of the greatest business books of all time). Level 5 is the pinnacle of leadership. It is the point at which you have developed leaders who are able and willing to develop other leaders. Level 5 leaders are fanatically driven for the purpose or mission of the company. Rather than being motivated to elevate their own status, they are passionate about making the company great. Very few leaders achieve this pinnacle.

Level 5 leaders:

→ Have and display humble confidence and humility

- → Develop leaders around themselves and set them up for success
- → Focus on surrounding themselves with Rock Star A Players
- → Give out credit for successes and take accountability for failures
- → Confront the brutal facts about their organization head-on
- → Lead a culture of execution throughout the organization
- → Have an indomitable will

In the words of Jim Collins: "Level 5 leaders display a powerful mixture of personal humility and indomitable will. They're incredibly ambitious, but their ambition is first and foremost for the cause, for the organization and its purpose, not themselves."

Becoming Level 5 leaders ourselves and developing these leaders throughout our organizations should be a tremendous goal and aspiration for us all. Becoming a Level 5 leader, though, first requires becoming a Level 2 leader, then a Level 3 leader, and then a Level 4 leader. It takes a tremendous amount of work and effort to reach the pinnacle. Becoming an Elite world-class Level 5 leader is a choice. It is not easy, but it is a choice. Unfortunately, most leaders are still struggling to achieve Level 3 status, production (more about this below).

Over the years, we have identified that there are twenty-four consistent practices of highly productive leaders.

24 PRACTICES OF HIGHLY PRODUCTIVE LEADERS

1. Discipline and Building Habits
2. Do More Than You Ask of Others
3. Prioritization

4. Making Hard Decisions
5. Difficult Conversations
6. Critical Thinking
7. Accountability and Ownership
8. Preparation and Organization (Meetings, Issues, Discussions)
9. Organization and Action: Taking Notes and Laying Out Clear Action Items
10. Questioning. Asking Why? Digging Deeper
11. Embracing Conflict and Leading Change
12. Keeping Focus on Results
13. Positive Enthusiasm
14. Aligning
15. Listening
16. Speak Simply and Directly
17. Coaching
18. Teaching
19. Inspection of Expectations
20. Performance Feedback/Evaluation
21. Follow Through
22. Obtaining Buy-In
23. Collaboration
24. Emotional Fortitude

These are the consistent practices that highly productive leaders have mastered. Of course, not all highly productive leaders are masters in all twenty-four of these consistent practices, but typically they are very proficient at many of them.

I have found that many leaders, even in executive roles, often struggle with consistently executing and generating a high level of productivity individually and in their team. Leaders who do not consistently lead their team to produce results will struggle to achieve and remain at Level 3 leadership (production), let alone be able to move to Level 4 leadership (people development).

In other words, you cannot develop additional leaders until you consistently produce. Improving on these twenty-four leadership practices is the path to driving consistent productivity. At DLP, we have leadership trainings each month where our existing and future leaders assess themselves across the 24 Leadership Practices of Highly Productive Leaders. In addition, during our biannual performance evaluations, team members also rate themselves on these practices.

A copy of this quick twenty-four leadership practices assessment tool can be found on DLPElite.com.

CRITICAL LEADERSHIP SKILLS

Four of the most critical skills for an Elite World-Class Leader are relationship building, communication, execution, and decision making.

RELATIONSHIP BUILDING

In my experience, there are four keys to building great relationships: promise keeping, aggressive listening, being consistently compassionate, and truth telling.

Elite World-Class Leaders provide positive encouragement, critical and honest feedback, and ongoing coaching. Elite World-Class Leaders understand that leadership is about service to others. It means thinking about others before themselves.

Relationships are built on trust, and great leaders cultivate trust by acting with humility, by acknowledging the whole person, and when needed, helping others with their life issues as part of the professional development process. The adage "People do not care how much you know until they know how much you care" rings true.

COMMUNICATION

In order to build relationships, you must be committed to open communication, and that requires you to become proficient in the many forms of communication necessary to lead and influence others.

Often, executives think that leaders just have to be great at giving presentations and other types of "one to many" public types of speaking and communications. There is no doubt that being able to speak to large groups with energy, excitement, confidence, and passion is an important leadership skill and worth taking the time to develop. The more important communication skill, however, is being able to effectively communicate one-on-one. Leadership is developed through building relationships, and relationships happen on a person-to-person level.

ACHIEVING ALIGNMENT

There are three communication components to creating great one-on-one relationships: listening, coaching, and fostering accountability. One of the best ways to build relationships and engage in all three is through the discipline of regular one-on-one meetings with each team member who reports to you. At DLP, we call these meetings alignment meetings.

During alignment meetings, we do not talk about the day-to-day whirlwind of projects, tasks, and clients that consume each and every workday. Instead, alignment meetings are a time to shift the focus specifically to the team member.

The alignment meeting starts with encouraging team members to share their successes and their challenges both professionally and personally. It requires active listening where you, as the leader, lean in and pay attention. This is an opportunity to truly get to know your team member and to show that you care, to display genuine compassion for their challenges and excitement for their possibilities and successes.

This alignment meeting also provides a great opportunity to coach the team member as you help them solve their problems and remove barriers to achieving their goals. By providing direct, clear, and concise feedback and advice on what the team member must improve upon, you are encouraging them to be more accountable, both to themselves and to the organization.

At DLP, we have found these meetings to be invaluable. The vast majority of people want to do a good job, and if given clear direction training and accountability, they will perform. I will go so far as to say that if you find that your teams and team members are ineffective, you can blame a lack of alignment and the failure to foster clear accountability as the primary culprit.

STORYTELLING

Whether you are communicating one-on-one or one-to-many, storytelling is a critical skill to develop if you are to communicate effectively. We all love to hear stories, so it should come as no surprise that people are much more engaged and usually learn better when information is presented through stories, rather than pure data or a list of facts. Stories appeal to emotions, and that, in turn, makes them much more memorable.

Try to use stories whenever you can—to deliver a message, make a point, or to teach. You will find this enhances your ability to communicate one-on-one with a team member, when speaking to a larger internal team, as well as to external audiences. Storytelling should be a staple part of your marketing messaging and in your sales presentations. If you are interested in exploring more about how storytelling enhances communications, Paul Smith has written two excellent books on this topic: *Lead with a Story* and *Sell with a Story*. I highly recommend both.

SPEAKING CLEARLY

A great leader must develop the ability to speak clearly and directly both one-on-one and to a larger audience. In my experience, I have found that some of the smartest people I know tend to struggle with this. They utilize too much "MBA talk."

As we discussed earlier, at DLP, we consider it the leader's job to make things easy for their team members. In order to do this, they must be able to clearly articulate a point or message. Using big words or providing long detailed instructions will only end up confusing people or, at the very least, losing their attention.

Brevity plays a large role in commanding people's interest and attention. The first time I heard the quote "If I had more time, I would have written a shorter letter," I knew it rang true. It is harder to deliver a message clearly and concisely than to ramble on. It takes more time to prepare a training, a presentation, or a message that is short and concise than one that is long and scattered.

COMMUNICATION TAKES TWO

Finally, I want to mention that Elite World-Class Leaders know that communication is a two-way street. They encourage critical feedback from their reports and team members so they can continue to grow and improve, including providing forums and real opportunities for team members to express their honest opinions.

At DLP, we do a few surveys each year that we send out to the whole organization seeking their feedback on what we are doing well, where we need to improve, and so on. We typically give them the option of putting their name on the survey or keeping their feedback anonymous.

One of our best surveys is called the Leadership Alignment Survey, where we seek feedback on if the team member feels aligned with our core values, their leader, the head of the division, and me. We also ask for feedback on how we are doing as leaders, how they feel about the workplace, if we are treating them with respect, if they feel valued, and many other questions that assess our job as leaders. A copy of this survey is available on DLPElite.com.

EXECUTION

The DLP definition of execution is getting things done (GTD).

If you cannot consistently get things done directly and through your team, you're going to have a hard time getting your team to follow your lead. Your team will not "follow you into battle" if you consistently come up short. If you do not have the ability to lead your team to achieve your goals, their confidence will be shaken and they will not have the same conviction and put in the same effort to achieve the next big goal.

This means doing what you say you are going to do, *always*. This means holding yourself accountable for results in the same manner as you hold your team members accountable for results.

This applies not only to being accountable and consistently executing on organizational priorities and projects, but it also applies to executing on the commitments you have made to your team members individually, including the commitments to provide them with clear communication and accountability. This is one of the key ways you help them grow and develop. Elite World-Class Leaders are responsible for executing. John Maxwell puts it this way: "Leadership is taking responsibility while others are making excuses." In other words, leaders face the music even when they don't like the tune. Leaders are accountable for results, both good and bad. They set the scene so the team can execute.

DECISION MAKING

Effective world-class leadership requires decision making, which stems from the ability to think critically. Critical thinkers have the ability to see enough of the whole picture to identify the root of a problem and then build a solution. One of the most important jobs of a great leader is to simplify the complex, to make things easy so that the team can execute. Everyone who exercises a leadership role at DLP understands this concept. It is our job to take the pressure on ourselves to make the hard decisions so the people who report to us can do their jobs unencumbered. Leaders learn how to give team members a voice and gather up opinions, insights, and feedback from their team, but know at the end of the day that they must be willing and able to make the decision.

DEVELOP AN OWNER'S MENTALITY

Just as a business owner is not necessarily a great leader, a great leader does not have to be an actual owner. But an Elite World-Class Leader does need to have an owner's mentality.

An owner's mentality is a focus on taking action—it is an aversion to internal politics and bureaucracy, and a focus on the bottom line and cash flow. This requires the willingness and requirement to hold themselves and their team accountable for achieving the desired result or expectation. They do this through empowerment, relationship building, and inspecting what they expect.

In addition, having an owner's mentality is an obsession with the front line. Remembering that the customer or client is first. Understanding that the experience you deliver to your customers is extremely critical for the ongoing success of the organization. This requires investing in your front line. Investing in hiring great A players in frontline roles, training them, making the expectations clear, and consistently being involved in the frontline customer experience. Great leaders cannot just sit in their comfy office and accept second- or thirdhand information. They must get out and interact with customers, get into the field, spend time with the frontline team members, shadow and inspect phone calls and emails between team members and customers. Pay close attention to negative reviews and be invested in changing what is causing the negative reviews and do everything possible to address each upset or disappointed customer's problem. Getting involved directly with these issues at least from time to time is a good thing. Having your feet in the dirt and actually experiencing your company's short falls or areas for improvement firsthand is really powerful.

An owner's mentality is also reflected in an understanding of how difficult it is to lead. Great leaders support their fellow leaders verbally and through action. There is cooperation, not competition. What affects one leader impacts all leaders. When one leader is trying to solve a problem, deliver a message, change a habit or process, it is critical that other leaders within the organization show support, even if it is not their top priority and even if they do not 100 percent agree with the decision or initiative.

We all like our own ideas more than we like the ideas of others. It is easier to be passionate for your idea or initiative than it is to have that same passion for someone else's idea. As CEO in my organization, if I push a new initiative and make it top priority, and then leaders tell their team members "Don't worry about that" or simply do not show support for the initiative, it will often be dead in the water. This is why leaders must support fellow leaders.

LEADERS CREATE LEADERS

As you work on developing the skills you need to become an

Elite World-Class Leader, you will start to see a change in behavior from the people around you. You will find that they are eager for someone to follow and that they are actually expecting you to lead. They will seek you out for help and advice, and this can produce its own set of new pressures. The good news is that one of the perks of becoming a great leader is that you will begin to share your responsibilities with those you nurture into leadership roles.

The more people you can elevate into leadership roles, the more responsibilities you can delegate and the less pressure you will feel. You will finally be able to move forward with all those plans for scaling your business because you know that you have developed a strong management team that can carry on the day-to-day aspects of the business that have taken up so much of your time.

Of course, this leadership chain reaction will not occur overnight. You begin the process of sharing responsibility by teaching others what you know. Mark Miller advises that after you have defined what leadership means in your company and you have shared that with your team members, you should then focus on ensuring that current and future leaders in your company have a way to acquire the skills they need to succeed.

Because we have a culture of leadership at DLP, we have adopted the mantra: *Leaders made here.*

This means that we are routinely and systematically developing leaders so we have a surplus of people ready for the next opportunity or challenge that comes up as we expand DLP. In other words, we are constantly building bench strength.

Focus on your future leaders, your "high potentials." Develop and offer them a clear training program so they can grow as leaders. Invest in them. Make it known to everyone in your organization how much you appreciate these team members and that you want to help develop them as future leaders.

An important part of the process of creating a place where "leaders are made" is the commitment to providing real opportunities for people to stretch and improve. We all suffer from the natural tendency to avoid risk, to fall back on the tried and true. In my own organization, we were guilty of falling back on the known, which meant that we were failing to give new leaders a shot at success or even at failure, which is also an important aspect of becoming a leader.

Typically, when a new project would come along, the leader responsible would assign someone seasoned, figuring it was better to be safe than sorry. Existing leaders rarely gave an emerging or inexperienced leader a shot. This did nothing to help young leaders grow and develop in a real-world setting. This safety-first mentality held us back. How could we continue to grow exponentially if we weren't letting our emerging leaders take on new responsibilities?

Developing and then, in turn, leading leaders is a much greater challenge than the challenge of leading followers or doers. When you develop leaders, you are nurturing people who will be leading others. In order to succeed at this, your leadership culture and approach must be strong enough, clear enough, and prioritized enough so that new leaders can be supported throughout the organization. Since leaders develop through one-on-one relationships, if you are not personally involved in each team member's road to leadership, you must count on your other leaders to mentor and nurture them, and that can prove challenging.

As you develop leaders who report to you, you will need to spend much of your one-on-one time with them coaching and training on how to lead their reports.

John Maxwell has developed the 3 Es of Leadership Development: environment, equipping, and exposure.

ENVIRONMENT

You may have heard the old saying, *Leadership is more caught than taught.*

This means that if you are leading from the front and by example, people will learn more from observing and experiencing your leadership than from any formal leadership training. They will not just be observing you but also the culture and environment that exists throughout the organization.

People acclimate themselves to whatever environment they are presented with. They will take their cues from subtle cultural messages that permeate the workplace. These unspoken messages shape your organization more than you might realize. Be attentive to these hidden messages that come from how people interact with each other. What is the prevailing emotional tone around the office? How intellectually stimulated are your team members? Look at the environment and assess whether it is conducive to creating the future leaders in your company.

EQUIPPING

The idea behind equipping is that leadership can be learned, and leaders can multiply their influence and a company's overall results by equipping others with the skills and confidence needed to become independent leaders. The future leader actually jumps into the task, preceded by proper training and followed by meaningful assessment and feedback.

Equipping is a process that can be broken down into five steps:

→ Say it by explaining the task
→ Show it by demonstrating how to perform the task
→ Assign it and let the person attempt the task
→ Study it by observing how the person performs the task
→ Assess it by offering feedback based on the leadership trainee's performance

EXPOSURE

While equipping focuses on deliverables, exposure focuses on vision, painting a picture of what successful leadership looks like. The premise here is that a little real-life exposure is better than a lot of theory. Exposure occurs through interaction and relationships with other strong leaders, whether that be fellow colleagues, industry experts, or external professional networks. You can create exposure within an organization by developing mentorship opportunities, creating internal leadership networks, and allowing and promoting informal learning opportunities. Make sure your leaders are also learning from their peers and from client feedback.

At DLP, one of the ways in which we have created exposure is by launching an internal Elite Leadership Program or ELP for short. This is a group of what we refer to as our "high potentials" or future leaders. Each member is assigned a mentor, who is often not in their reporting chain and whose sole focus is mentoring the ELP member. We provide formal leadership training, problem solving in small groups, and stretch projects. We've also developed a peer network of ELP members who otherwise may have had limited interaction with one another due to roles in different business units and offices.

LEADERSHIP RESOURCES AND TOOLS

I am continuously studying leadership. I am constantly learning and evolving my own leadership style and incorporating new insights into my company's growth paradigm.

Although I have lost count of all of the leadership books I have read over the years, the following seventeen titles have significantly impacted my own journey of becoming an Elite World-Class Leader, and I highly recommend each one:

→ *The Five Levels of Leadership* by John Maxwell
→ *The Coaching Habit* by Michael Stanier
→ *Leadership and Self-Deception* by the Arbinger Institute
→ *Dare to Lead* by Brené Brown
→ *Leaders Made Here* by Mark Miller
→ *Lead with a Story* by Paul Smith
→ *Leadership Wisdom* by Robin Sharma
→ *How to Be a Great Boss* by Gino Wickman
→ *The Monk Who Sold His Ferrari* by Robin Sharma
→ *The Leader Who Had No Title* by Robin Sharma
→ *Leading Change* by John Kotter
→ *Decisive: How to Make Better Choices at Life and Work* by Chip Heath

- → *Good Leaders Ask Great Questions* by John Maxwell
- → *Speak like Churchill, Stand like Lincoln* by James Humes
- → *21 Irrefutable Laws of Leadership* by John Maxwell
- → *The Trillion Dollar Coach* by Eric Schmidt
- → *The Servant* by James C. Hunt

More information about these titles can be found at DLPElite. com, along with additional leadership tools.

LIVING FULLY: WORK-LIFE INTEGRATION

Elite World-Class Leaders live fully, integrating work and life holistically. They do this through discipline, by building habits and rituals that free up their time and allow them to focus on what really matters. They give up short-term pleasures in order to realize greater achievement and fulfillment.

Elite World-Class Leaders apply these principles to all parts of their lives—in work, family, faith, and any other area of importance. It is important as a leader that you show your team that you genuinely live a full life because you want your team members to also live full lives, and you must lead by example. As much as you want them to work hard and give their all, you also want to encourage them to be great wives or husbands, to be great parents, to be involved in their faith, and to invest in anything else that is important to them.

You want everyone in your company to have passions outside of work. People who feel they are successful in each area of their lives are going to be happier, more engaged, and will deliver better work. They are going to be better leaders. As a leader, it is your responsibility to invest in your people and support them in being the best they can be in all areas of their lives.

As long as you build and maintain a culture that includes encouraging and supporting all your leaders and team members, you will be in a much better position to weather any storm and mitigate any risks your company might face.

CHAPTER FIVE

UNDERSTANDING AND MITIGATING RISKS

More companies go bankrupt due to growth than a lack of growth. That may sound surprising, but it is a fact.

In the early years of an enterprise—during the time your idea is first being transformed into an actual profitable company—your focus has to be on day-to-day issues such as making payroll or how to manage the company's marketing spend in the face of revenue fluctuations. Your owner's mentality, your frontline obsession, and your laser focus on the customer experience drive you to form tight connections with the people and projects that make your business a success. You oversee all operations, participate in every meeting, and have the final say when it comes to hiring decisions.

Then you start to grow.

You form layers of middle managers; you bring on human resources professionals; you create pages of policies and procedures; and you invest in infrastructure and technology. As this bureaucracy forms, you start moving away from what drove your success in the first place. You find yourself turning your focus away from managing internal matters and personal issues and, instead, start listening to outside noise. Eventually, you find yourself in a situation where you are putting more focus on trying to understand and mitigate perceived external risks that could impact your growing enterprise than on the business itself.

What if there is a recession?

What if the outcome of the next presidential election means more taxes?

What if there is a regulatory change?

What if there is a sudden drop in the stock market?

How could a continuing trade war with China affect business?

What if Amazon or Facebook or one of the other big technology companies comes in and changes the business landscape and makes our model obsolete?

Although the economic, political, global, and technological environments are all factors that can indeed affect your business, these external concerns are not what puts your business at the most risk. Yes, you should be aware of external changes that could affect your business, but you should not let that be your primary focus. You should not adjust your day-to-day actions based on emotions, on your fears of what could happen.

Focusing your energy on mitigating the risks external to your business is important, but I think we have all learned through COVID-19 that there are going to be things we cannot predict. You must accept that there are external unknowns you cannot possibly prepare for and instead recognize that the biggest risk to the survival, growth, and health of your business is not external; it is internal.

Most of the risk your organization faces revolves around the dangers that result from lacking the right disciplines. When turbulence, volatility, and recessions hit, such as COVID-19, it is the most disciplined and strongest businesses in each industry that thrive, while the weaker companies will fight for survival—and many will, unfortunately, fail.

DISCIPLINE TRUMPS RECESSION

A significant percentage of the world's wealthiest individuals created the majority of their wealth during the 15 to 20 percent of the time that we're in a recessionary environment. The other 80 to 85 percent of the time, we are in a strong and growing economy. So if you find yourself worrying about whether we are heading into a recession that is going to put you out of business, you are wasting your time. If we are not in a recession, we are always moving toward a recession, but they do not last long.

What could put you out of business, though, is the failure to establish enough discipline into your company's operations to weather a recession (or capitalize on it, as world-class organizations do), transcend a trade war, or survive a term or two of whoever occupies the Oval Office.

DISCIPLINE AND FAILURE

As discussed previously, successfully adhering to the quadrants of the Elite Execution System comes down to discipline: disciplined thought, disciplined people, and disciplined action. Companies that fail have typically lost sight of discipline in all three of those areas.

Don't be lulled into a false sense of security just because your sales are strong and revenue is up. These are not the only factors to consider when determining if your company is ready for growth and prepared for market corrections. The effects that lack of discipline have on a company—a bureaucracy that takes on a life of its own and a workforce that is getting fat and lazy—can creep up on you slowly.

In his book *How the Mighty Fail*, Jim Collins does an amazing job breaking down the five stages of a company in failure.

Stage one is what he calls hubris born of success. This occurs when great companies lose sight of what actually drove their success. They start saying things such as, "We're successful because we do these things," instead of saying, "We're successful because *we understand why* we do these specific things." They become filled with hubris, assuming everything that they do will be successful because everything they have done so far has been successful.

Collins calls stage two of a company in failure "the undisciplined pursuit of more." These businesses, because they have succeeded in one or more sectors, are tempted to tackle additional opportunities, spreading their limited resources of money, time, attention, and people to new business ventures. This overreaching causes them to struggle to do anything with excellence because they are trying to do so many different things. As they jump into new businesses and change course and direction, they lose sight of their core values, their purpose, and their mission.

These companies forget the wise adage that true success comes from saying no to many very good ideas in favor of a few really great ideas. In other words, less really is more.

Stage three is the denial of risk and peril. Companies moving into stage three ignore the warning signs that things are starting to veer off course. Their leaders say things such as, *It's not that bad. Nothing is fundamentally wrong. It was just a bad quarter or two. The market was soft. Everyone struggled over that period.* These are all attempts to explain away disturbing data, writing them off as temporary anomalies. They not only discount negative indicators, but they also ramp up the positive spin on everything they can, hoping to drown out any negative noise. Any setbacks can be explained away with external factors because after all, nothing is the company's fault.

Although during bad markets these businesses are quick to blame the down economy for their troubles, they will also find ways to come up with stage three excuses during a great market. Their leaders say things such as, *Well, there's just so much competition out there; it's hard to find great deals. Right now, marketing is really expensive because everyone is competing for the same ads. All the great people have lots of job opportunities, so that's why we are struggling to hire great people and why our payroll is so high.*

Is it any wonder that more businesses fail during a strong market than during a weak one?

Whether the economy is good or bad, you are always going to be able to find external excuses for your business's decline. And whether the economy is good or bad, the real reasons behind your business problems are always going to be internal.

When a company is in stage four of failure, it begins a really sharp decline and starts grasping for salvation. The critical question for these companies becomes, how will the leadership respond? It is very challenging for a company to turn itself around at this stage. There has to be a radical transformation. Only a strong visionary leader with a bold strategy that includes a dramatic increase of accountability has any chance of pulling it off.

Finally, stage five of business failure is capitulation to irrelevance or death. If a company reaches this point, it is merely struggling to survive. It's highly unlikely the business can turn around.

I encourage you to think about these five stages in terms of how your own business is performing and ask yourself if you are in any of these stages now. Pay attention to the possibility of hubris. Be honest with yourself if you find you are starting to go down a path of the undisciplined pursuit of more or are falling into the trap of denial of risk. As long as you are not in one of the last stages, you still have time to turn things around. The way to start is to recognize that all risks are internal and then set in motion a method to identify and measure the real risks that could endanger your company's ability to grow.

MEASURE PRODUCTIVITY TO INCREASE PRODUCTIVITY

Convinced that the real risks our business faces are internal, we have spent a lot of time at DLP working through the challenge of how to measure the strength of our company. We have consistently grown between 50 and 80 percent each year, because early on we understood the importance of making sure we have the internal discipline to sustain this level of rapid expansion.

We developed a way to measure the strength of our organization and to what extent we can withstand anything that comes at us. This measurement is what we call productivity per person or PPP.

To establish PPP, we take our net revenue (gross revenue minus cost of goods sold) and divide it by our total number of team members. We then track that number over a trailing twelve months. So every month, we pull a trailing twelve-month report tracking our net revenue each month for the previous twelve months and the number of team members we had each month during that time. This gives us our PPP number. If you are willing to share your net profit with your entire organization, I believe tracking net profits instead of net revenue is an even better indicator, but that will require full transparency of your financials to the entire business.

When DLP started this tracking a few years ago, our PPP was $108,500 per person for the previous twelve months. At that point, that number did not tell us much, other than that was the starting point for our analysis. We had no way of knowing if it was a good number or not. That number became our baseline, and the goal became trying to improve upon it, to become more productive per person as we became bigger.

We use the PPP as a gauge of business strength and a litmus test for whether we are growing the right way and becoming stronger. Say, for example, that your organization is doing $10 million in net revenue, and you have a hundred people in your organization. That would mean you have a baseline of $100,000 PPP. Over the next two years, let's say you grow your net revenue from $10 million to $15 million. If you are just looking at that one metric—net revenue—it's easy to conclude that your business is strong and healthy. After all, you grew your revenue by 50 percent. But what if, in order to reach that $15 million mark, you went from a staff of 100 people to 250? If you divide $15 million by 250, you go down to $60,000 per person. Even though your net revenue went up by 50 percent, your number of people went up by 250 percent, meaning you're actually earning 40 percent less per person than you were when you were 50 percent smaller. If you find yourself heading in a similar direction, you are not on a scalable path of growth. Scaling the Elite Execution System way is high growth AND high profit. The fact that it is taking significantly more resources to achieve significant growth is a sign that you are building bureaucracy and, at the same time, diminishing your ability to execute. This is an indication that your company is at risk.

After our first year of tracking PPP at DLP, we had added a total of seventy-three new team members while increasing our productivity per person from $108,500 to over $131,000. That was a 23 percent increase in productivity per person. Instead of just looking at our increase in net revenue and wondering whether we were actually in good shape, we were able to conclude that our rise in revenue was accompanied by a rise in productivity, allowing us to proceed with executing our growth plans.

At DLP, we continue to track our PPP every month, pulling an updated T12 so we can see how we are faring as we bring on additional resources to handle our business expansion.

There was a time this past year that our PPP declined for two straight months, something that had never happened before at DLP. This set off alarm bells to me and DLP's entire leadership team, leading us to drive corrective actions throughout the organization. We focused on encouraging each team member to develop an owner's mentality, making this our quarterly theme and even holding a big company-wide contest around it. We focused on resolving C players. We focused on accountability. We made sure everyone in the organization was aware of the PPP setbacks and focused on driving individual and, in turn, company productivity. In just three months, we were able to realize a PPP increase of more than 15 percent.

ENCOURAGING TEAM MEMBER BUY-IN

The first time that we told our team members that we were targeting a 28 percent increase in productivity for the year, they thought we were crazy. Management was bombarded with questions from team members: *How can we become 28 percent more productive? I'm already working fifty or sixty hours a week. How am I possibly going to become almost 30 percent more productive?*

We understood this reaction, but we also believed that together we could make this happen.

The key to team member buy-in was making sure each team member felt that he or she was also benefiting and directly connected to this initiative and focus. Of course, operating a business with a strong foundation, with the ability to withstand market changes and other external risks, and that is growing and becoming more profitable will benefit everyone. As long as your business is thriving, your team members will have jobs and opportunities for advancement.

Continuing to collect a paycheck, however, was not by itself going to provide enough incentive for frontline associates to affirmatively seek out ways to increase productivity. We needed to provide a more tangible and direct reason as to why working toward greater company productivity would benefit each team member. We needed to make it personal.

We came up with the idea of tying the PPP goals to our company 401(k) team member retirement program. Up until this time, we had always operated our 401(k) program with a 50 percent company match. If a team member contributed 5 percent of their salary to the 401(k), we matched it at 2.5 percent.

Now with the new 28 percent PPP program goal, we decided to increase our 401(k) match incrementally in proportion to whether and to what extent the productivity goal was met. If the company achieves a 7 percent increase in productivity, we increase everybody's company match from 50 percent to 60 percent. If we achieve a 14 percent increase in productivity, we increase the amount of the company match to 70 percent. At a 21 percent increase in productivity, that match goes up to 80 percent. And if we hit our goal of a 28 percent increase in PPP, each person contributing to the 401(k) program receives a 100 percent company match. This, effectively, amounts to a

2.5 percent salary increase for everyone in the company who chooses to participate.

What we were proposing was real money for each and every team member, and we made this a prime human resources focus throughout the organization. The 28 percent increase in PPP was mentioned in every meeting; we created dashboards and scorecards so people could see the data displayed around the office. Productivity per person became something that everybody in the company was aware of, was concerned with, and was paying attention to.

We started doing a lot of training around how to drive individual productivity. We designed programs to help our team members learn how to think creatively when faced with the prospect of adding more people, resources, or expenses.

EVERYONE DRIVES REVENUE

At DLP, we train our team members to constantly consider ways to drive revenue, even if they are not in sales. Every DLP team member—from our service techs to our receptionists to our accountants—understand how they can help drive revenue, generate referrals, find opportunities, garner repeat business, and collect money due to us, to name just a few examples. In addition, we teach every team member—through training and by sharing examples and success stories—how they can cut expenses. We encourage team members to continuously consider how finding new vendors, renegotiating with vendors, cutting waste, and getting more done with less people can help with efficiency and execution. By rallying our team members behind increasing productivity and faithfully tracking it every month, increasing productivity now drives each team member's individual decisions. It literally has changed the way our team members view and perform in their jobs.

For example, let's say every member of a five-person team feels overworked and overwhelmed. The typical response in most organizations is for those five team members to lobby for the hiring of a sixth team member to help ease the pressure.

But if you have a culture where the focus is on increasing the company's overall productivity per person, that team's going to be thinking, "Well, if we add another person, that's going to decrease our productivity by 15 or 20 percent." Instead, they're going to work to find ways to increase their efficiencies. They will look for ways to drive the process better, to leverage technology, to maximize effort in more effective ways.

Making more money is not the only incentive we gave our team members to increase productivity. We also found ways to use the PPP program to enhance team member engagement while appealing to their good hearts and desire to give back to the community.

DLP runs a nonprofit foundation called the DLP Positive Returns Foundation. We focus on helping people dream bigger, live better, and choose prosperity. The focus is centered on education, jobs, and affordable housing. Many of our team members and I share a passion for these causes. When thinking about how to get team members excited about the PPP program while also promoting better overall team member engagement, we came up with the idea of layering in contributions to the foundation on behalf of the team members. Depending on the percentage of PPP realized, the company increases its donation on behalf of our team members. The closer we get to the goal, the more money we donate to the foundation. If we hit our goal of a 28 percent PPP increase, at the end of the year, the company donates an additional $50,000 to the foundation on behalf of our team members. This is in addition to DLP's giving policy mentioned in chapter 2, which is 1 percent of our time, ¼ percent of all of our net revenue, and ¼ percent of all capital we raise.

Increasing the company's productivity has become a source of pride for our team members because not only are they benefiting themselves and their families with our increased contributions to their 401(k)s, but their commitment also truly makes an impact on the lives of many who are in need of a hand up. Interested team members can even join a charity committee to help run the foundation and direct where the money goes. Coming together to pursue the greater good motivates our team members and propels us all to do our best to reach our goals.

When you can get your organization behind and focused on driving productivity and it enters your collective consciousness, your team can accomplish tremendous feats. The compounding effect can be mind-boggling.

In DLP's case, we are looking at jumping from $108,000 in PPP just a few years ago to realizing a million dollars per person in just a few years. And it all came about because we set that initial baseline, measured our monthly progress, and rallied our team members around the fact that increasing productivity reduces risk and benefits everyone.

ENCOURAGING TEAM MEMBER ENGAGEMENT

Disengagement at work is the number one challenge to a company's profitability. Disengagement fuels unproductive behaviors. Instead of giving their all to projects and priorities, disengaged team members do whatever they can to skate through their days. They spend their time text messaging, checking Facebook, surfing the internet, and just doing enough to keep their job. Disengagement is an epidemic in the American workforce. I recently read a Gallup study that found that 72 percent of US employees are not engaged at work. That is simply astounding to me. Think about it—nearly three out of four people are not engaged. Does it now make better sense why it feels like you have a small group of superheroes in your business who drive most of the results, while almost everyone else seems happy to sit back?

Disengaged team members are also a problem because they negatively affect your Rock Star A Players, causing them to become worn out over time as they continue to carry more weight than their fellow team members.

Measuring PPP has the added benefit of being a great way to measure team member engagement. You cannot grow fast and increase profitability if your team members are disengaged. While you may be able to do so for the short term as long as you have some really great superheroes putting forth herculean efforts day in and day out, that can only cover up for disengaged team members who are not accountable for driving real results for so long.

C PLAYERS

C players are the downfall of many organizations. C players

generally fall into two categories: people whose behaviors do not match your core values and people who do not execute and achieve the desired results of the role. In other words, C players are generally either not great producers or they are not great team members. If someone falls into both of these categories, that would make them a D player. Hopefully, you do not have any D players in your organization.

Not every underperforming team member is doomed to remain a C player. Sometimes team members become disengaged because they are not being challenged or because there is a lack of leadership. They are not being given opportunities or being held accountable. These are the people who, while currently not performing, could become highly productive and engaged if provided with better structure, training, and accountability.

In addition, people may not be engaged or productive because they are simply in the wrong seat within the organization. Maybe they are a great fit for the organization's culture—people might even love them—but they are not driving results yet. That could all change if you moved them into the right role with the right responsibilities and expectations.

More often than not, however, your C players are not going to change. The simple truth is that you cannot run a business loaded up with C players if you want to be able to weather whatever storms come your way. You cannot grow profitability over the long term with average or lower-than-average team members.

We sometimes keep C players on because either they do the job really well but are not a cultural fit, or they are a great cultural fit but cannot do the job. Either situation exposes your organization to significant risk.

The people who are not cultural fits—the ones whose behaviors do not match your core values and who are not good team-mates—can create significant risks for many reasons. Common examples of this are people who always put themselves first and are egocentric. They focus first on what is best for them, not what is best for the organization, and may even make choices that are good for them but bad for the business or your clients. As your company grows, you are exposed to more and more risk of theft, fraud, and other material financial risk. Although not every C or D player is going to be a thief, another big risk these toxic people present is the reputational risk that comes with how they treat your clients, partners, and vendors. This is especially a problem if you have these types of people in leadership seats.

Toxic people can result in your A players becoming less pro-ductive or, even worse, leaving your organization altogether. If you have ever had one of these negative personalities on a team with you and felt like you would rather be anywhere than in a meeting with this person or otherwise having to deal with them, then you know the kind of person I am talking about. Do not put up with the wrong people in your organization even if they are extremely talented and individually produc-tive. The cost ends up being just too high. I encourage you to use the chug test in your company and in life. If you have someone in your organization or someone you are debating adding, evaluate them based on this simple test. Ask yourself, "Would I want to go grab a beer with this person after work?" If that answer is "Heck no, I would not want to spend time hanging out with this person," then that person is very likely not the type of individual you should have working for you.

The second type of C player—the cultural fit who cannot seem to "get the ball in the hoop"—can be nearly as large of a risk. You can't allow people who are unable to consistently generate results occupy seats within your organization because, frankly, they can create many of the same types of risks that dishonest or "me first" people create. When you have people in your company who have consistently proven that they cannot be counted on to produce results, you are in turn exposing yourself to tremendous risk. When team members fail to generate results, they drag down revenue, profits, and growth, and they put significantly more pressure on you and your best people. This additional pressure on your A players will frustrate them and, in turn, can result in you losing your very best people.

Finally, perhaps the most significant risk that comes with having C players occupy seats is that they represent lost opportunities for filling those seats with Rock Star A Players who will drive your organization forward as they generate profits, bring in big relationships, and attract more A players.

MITIGATING RISK WITH A PLAYERS

In order to become an Elite Organization that mitigates risks and embraces opportunities, you must fill all seats with A players. In fact, your primary focus must be on building a disciplined culture filled with A players, one that has an extreme bias toward action and execution with an emphasis on the development of leaders. You must have leaders who have an owner's mentality and insist on an obsession with the front line throughout the organization.

If you can do this while staying humble, avoiding hubris, and also incorporating a clear metric such as PPP into your organization to measure productivity, you will not only be in a position to grow and prosper in good times, but you will also be in a great position to actually capitalize on volatility, uncertainty, and market corrections.

Of course, mitigating risks is not enough to get you the results you need to transform into an Elite Organization. You need to move forward, consistently and with discipline, day after day. You need to commit to a 20-Mile March.

CHAPTER SIX

THE 20-MILE MARCH

In chapter 2, "The Elite Compass," I championed the concept of having a secret weapon to maintain a company's health and direct its growth. As I explained then, DLP's secret weapon is the 20-Mile March, a systematic disciplined approach to consistent growth year over year regardless of the market, the economy, or any other outside influences.

Because I believe in its powers so much, I have made the 20-Mile March an integral part of the Elite Execution System. I place so much emphasis on the 20-Mile March because I am convinced that had DLP not adopted this approach years ago, we would not have realized a fraction of the success and growth we have achieved. Without incorporating its principles each day into our operations and our strategy, the DLP team would certainly not have been able to grow the business as rapidly and consistently as we have over the last ten-plus years.

THE 20-MILE MARCH STORY

Jim Collins introduced the 20-Mile March concept in his book *Great by Choice*. In the best-selling book, he tells the true story of two expedition crews that set out to be the first ever to reach the South Pole in a harrowing 1,400-mile journey across unknown and treacherous terrain in, at times, 20-degree-below-zero temperatures. The team that arrived first made its return journey home safely. The other team reached the South Pole thirty-four days later but, tragically, never made it home. The difference between these two teams was the successful team took the 20-Mile March approach, whereas the other did not.

After a significant amount of research, Collins concluded that all great companies have one thing in common: they adhere to the 20-Mile March.

When I explain the 20-Mile March, I like to present it as a less chilling but equally effective parable. If you are listening to the audio version of this book, I encourage you to find a quiet place where you can just sit back and listen for a moment without distraction. If you are driving, please pull over to a safe place, put your car in park, close your eyes, and listen.

> Imagine you and a competitor are both standing with your feet in the Pacific Ocean in San Diego, looking inland. You are about to embark on a three thousand mile walk from where you stand to the tip of Maine. You are both excited and energized to be taking this momentous journey. The challenge is to see who can reach Maine first.
>
> On the first day, you hike twenty miles, making it to the edge of town. You feel pretty good. You pitch your tent, have a meal, settle in, and enjoy a great night's sleep.
>
> On the second day, you march another twenty miles, still enjoy-

ing the beautiful weather. On the third day, you march your twenty miles, but now you have reached the heat of the desert. It's stifling, more than one hundred degrees, and you feel dehydrated and worn down. You laugh at how people dismiss the harsh desert heat as *only a dry heat*. It's becoming almost unbearable, and with every step you are fighting the urge to stop and set up camp so you can dive into your tent to get away from the relentless sun. You push through, though, and complete your day's twenty-mile trek. Through sheer determination, you keep up this twenty-mile pace as you make your way through the desert day after day.

Finally, you hit friendlier terrain and cooler weather. The contrast is striking. You feel a surge of renewed energy. The wind is at your back. You know that you are capable of marching many more than twenty miles now, but you stay the course; you hold back; you modulate your pace. You continue on your steady march for the rest of your journey, walking precisely twenty miles each day, no more and no less. You push through when the weather is harsh, and you feel grateful when conditions are favorable so you can complete your miles early and rest. You reach Maine a happy and healthy person, rejuvenated from the adventure and with energy to spare.

Now, back to your competitor who was also at the shore of the Pacific Ocean in San Diego with the same trip before him. He has the same equipment as you do, the same map to guide him on his journey, and the same goal of reaching Maine first.

When he embarks on his march, the weather, of course, is also perfect—isn't it always in San Diego? He is excited and energized; he feels on top of the world! He puts in a great effort, completing forty miles on his very first day.

He's extremely proud of his progress but understandably exhausted. He pitches his tent, and when he wakes up, the desert sun is scorching. He lies back down in his cool tent, figuring that because he did such a great job the day before covering all those extra miles, he might as well hang out in his tent a while longer to avoid the hottest part of the day.

This scenario repeats itself, over and over. On good days, he marches with great enthusiasm until he cannot march anymore. On bad days, he hunkers down in his tent, waiting and whining about how the conditions aren't conducive to moving forward.

It's no surprise that he has fallen behind. He renews his resolve to pick up the pace again. Just before he hits the Colorado high mountains, he finds himself in a stretch of glorious weather. He goes all out, logging forty- to fifty-mile days to make up for lost ground. Then, while hiking through a particularly perilous patch of terrain, he hits a huge winter snowstorm. He makes it through and finally gets to a spot of relative safety where he can rest for the night. He makes camp and hunkers down. Still traumatized from the experience of navigating that treacherous trail, he decides to stay put until spring arrives.

When spring does finally arrive, he emerges physically weakened and psychologically defeated as he stumbles off in the direction of Maine. By the time he reaches Kansas City, you, with your relentless, consistent, disciplined twenty-mile-a-day march, have already reached the tip of Maine.

The point of the parable is this: Achieving long-term success and maintaining a high-growth AND high-profit business year after year requires incredible and consistent discipline, day after day. It means not allowing the conditions or influences of the outside world—whether they concern politics, the competition, or the economy, to name just a few—to dictate your decisions or distract you from putting forth relentless disciplined activity, day after day.

When I tell this parable to new team members in our monthly Welcome to DLP meeting, I always ask them, *What is the message of this story?* I usually get a response that goes something like, "Slow and steady wins the race," or "It's the story of the tortoise and the hare."

This response is partially accurate. The 20-Mile March does rely on consistent effort. But it is much more than that. If you have ever tracked your steps via a step tracking app such as a Fitbit, you can attest to the fact that walking or hiking twenty miles in a single day is a lot of activity; it's a massive amount of activity. This is the amount of activity I am talking about when I say we adhere to the 20-Mile March each and every day. We engage in massive amounts of activity *every single day*. We don't put forth this level of effort just on good days or on days where we have the time or on the days that we feel like it. The 20-Mile March is about everyone in the organization putting forth this level of consistent activity each day, every day. Not just for a week, or a month, but year after year after year.

BECOMING A 20-MILE MARCHER: THE 80/20 RULE

In order to put the 20-Mile March into tangible action on the business front, each member of your team must develop their own relentless, consistent focus on marching forward for that twenty miles each day.

To find out where that twenty-mile focus needs to be, it is

helpful to understand the 80/20 rule, also known as the Pareto principle.

The 80/20 rule states that 80 percent of results come from just 20 percent of actions. The rule applies to pretty much everything. For example, 80 percent of the world's traffic is concentrated on 20 percent of the world's roads; and 80 percent of the world's wealth is controlled by 20 percent of the world's population.

When it comes to individual productivity, 20 percent of a worker's activities produce 80 percent of their results. In other words, for somebody working a forty-hour work week, eight hours of that forty-hour week is producing 80 percent of their results. Even though some people may find it hard to believe that 80 percent of the value they bring to an organization comes from such a proportionately small amount of time, not only have many studies confirmed this, but I've personally observed it to be true over the course of many years working in several different industries.

What might be even more mind-boggling is that you can break this down even further. There is actually a 64/4 rule that is calculated this way: take the 20 percent of your time that produced 80 percent of your results and then apply the same 80/20 principle to it; or, in other words, apply the 80/20 principle to the second degree. You will find that 64 percent of your results come from just 20 percent of your most productive 20 percent of time. That means that just 4 percent of your time is producing nearly two thirds of your results.

To say it another way, 64 percent of your results each week are coming from only a few hours of your time. Now apply this to your entire workforce. It's easy to see why so much time seems to be spent getting so very little done.

The secret weapon part of this comes into focus when you figure out which activities are producing the greatest results. Then it's a simple matter of helping your team members look for ways to do more of the tasks that reap the greatest rewards.

Take, for example, a company's sales force. The most productive time for a salesperson is when they are engaged either in prospecting for new clients or when they are actually in front of a customer selling. You would think that a salesperson would spend the majority of their time engaged in these activities, especially since all or a significant portion of their compensation is tied to prospecting and selling. However, this is not going to be the case.

The reality is that the average salesperson who works fifty hours a week will spend only about two of those hours prospecting and maybe, at best, ten of them at sales appointments. The remaining thirty-eight hours of their week is going to be sucked up by other tasks, such as following up on customer service issues, completing paperwork, and attending meetings, all activities that produce zero sales. Very often, as salespeople start generating a moderate amount of success, they actually spend less and less time in sales appointments or prospecting and more of their time on this other less productive "busy work."

Almost everyone, regardless of their job, gets mired in administrative minutiae or caught up in these types of nonproductive day-to-day drills. Often, these tasks present themselves as urgent, as things that you feel you have to do right this minute. Even though these so-called urgent tasks are not part of your productive 20 percent, they will hijack your attention, your time, and your focus.

Recognizing this as a universal phenomenon in the workplace, at DLP, we focus on training our team members on the 80/20 principle, getting them to fully understand and embrace the 20-Mile March philosophy, and most importantly, helping them uncover which tasks produce their personal productive 20 percent. We are very clear about each team member's responsibilities and expectations, as we encourage them to come up with ways to spend more time on the right activities. The results from this approach have been astounding. As mentioned in the last chapter, we are on pace to triple our productivity per person in just a few short years.

THE DLP 20-MILE MARCH ROADMAP TO SUCCESS

To help our team members better focus their energies on the activities that produce results, we developed the *20-Mile March Roadmap to Success*, which is available on DLPElite.com. In this document, we present twenty different ways that team members can maximize their own individual productivity and drastically increase their results and achievements. The following provides an overview of the 20-Mile March Roadmap.

1. HAVE A PURPOSE

First, we encourage team members to understand why they do the things they do. We ask them to think about what they really want out of life and what they want out of their role in the organization.

This is really critical. As mentioned previously, over 70 percent of team members today are not engaged at work. If your team members are not actively engaged in the workplace, you will not be able to drive consistent growth. You will not be able to live the 20-Mile March.

The challenge to have a purpose is best illustrated by "The Lion Chaser Manifesto" taken from the book *Chase the Lion* by Mark Batterson, which we share with our team members in the Roadmap to Success. The quote reads:

> Quit living as if the purpose of life is to arrive safely at death. Run to the roar. Set God-sized goals. Pursue God-given passions. Go after a dream that is destined to fail without divine intervention. Stop pointing out problems. Become part of the solution. Stop repeating the past. Start creating the future. Face your fears. Fight for your dreams. Grab opportunity by the mane and don't let go! Live like today is the first day and last day of your life. Burn sinful bridges. Blaze new trails. Live for the applause of nail-scarred hands. Don't let what's wrong with you keep you from worshiping what's right with God. Dare to fail. Dare to be different. Quit holding out. Quit holding back. Quit running away.

A number of DLP team members use this quote as a screensaver or have it taped to their monitors or pinned to their bulletin boards. It seems to resonate with almost everyone as they work to develop greater purpose in their lives and in their work.

2. HAVE A PLAN AND CLEAR GOALS

One of my favorite quotes by Ben Franklin is, "By failing to prepare, you are preparing to fail."

It is important that team members not only understand the organization's plan and goals but that each one of them develops a personal and professional plan and sets goals for themselves. We offer tools and goal-setting exercises to help our team members evaluate their lives as a whole, setting clear goals for what they want to accomplish long term, midterm, and short term.

Each year, we help each team member complete a life assessment and goal-setting exercise to help them develop their ten- to twenty-five-year long-term goals, three- to five-year goals, as well as their top ten goals for the next year.

3. LIVE YOUR COMPANY'S CORE VALUES

When the behaviors and day-to-day actions of each team member align with and drive the core values of the company, productivity cannot help but follow. Lead by living the company core values, and your team will join you in common cause.

4. ACHIEVE YOUR ROCKS AND 5. ACHIEVE YOUR WIGS

I put numbers four and five, concerning Rocks and WIGs, together here because they will be covered in detail in chapters 7 and 8. In brief, Rocks are the specific personal and professional goals that each individual sets into motion each quarter, while WIGs, which stands for Wildly Important Goals, are the biggest and most important objectives established collectively by an entire team. Achieving Rocks and WIGs consistently is everything when growing a business.

6. INCREASE YOUR POSITIVITY

Jon Gordon, in his book *The Energy Bus: 10 Rules to Fuel Your Life, Work and Team with Positive Energy*, said, "Positive energy is like muscle. The more you use it, the stronger it gets."

I couldn't agree more. The kind of energy a team member gives off makes a remarkable difference to not only their own level of productivity but also to the behavior of the entire team. Negative energy drags everyone down, whereas positive energy fuels creativity and productivity. When Howard Schultz, the chairman and CEO of Starbucks, was asked how he gets all those baristas to smile so much, he answered, "It's simple. I hire people who like to smile."

At DLP, we don't expect that we can take a Debbie Downer and turn that person into a positive individual. Instead, we try to hire positive people and then promote the power and importance of positivity within our company, encouraging people to bring their highest energy and most optimistic selves to work each day.

7. BE ACCOUNTABLE AND HOLD YOUR TEAM MEMBERS ACCOUNTABLE

The Oz Principle defines accountability as "a personal choice to rise above one's circumstances and demonstrate the ownership necessary for achieving desired results." First expounded in the book *The Oz Principle: Getting Results through Individual and Organizational Accountability* by Roger Connors, Tom Smith, and Craig Hickman, the principle challenges people to be "above the line thinkers" who "See it. Own it. Solve it. Do it."

The Elite Execution System challenges everyone in the organization to live this principle of accountability in everything they do.

8. SOLVE ISSUES

This is best explained by the Elite Execution System's IDS method problem solving. IDS, covered in detail in chapter 9, stands for Identify, Discuss, and Solve.

9. PARTICIPATE IN DRIVEN FOR GREATNESS

Driven for Greatness, which is interchangeable with "seeking knowledge," is a DLP core value. We choose a book each month that we read together. These books are on a wide range of topics such as leadership, productivity, passion, purpose, speaking, storytelling, and habit building. Every other week, we get together to discuss the book in our Driven for Greatness meetings. Although this is explained in greater detail in chapter 9, I know from my own personal experience that getting people to actively expand their knowledge base is a big part of driving productivity.

10. GROW YOUR LEVEL OF LEADERSHIP

As discussed in chapter 4, leadership is central to success and productivity. At DLP, we focus on our leaders achieving Level 3 leadership: Production, and we put a tremendous focus on the twenty-four practices of highly productive leaders that we covered in chapter 4.

11. UTILIZE CHECKLISTS

Although encouraging team members to utilize checklists might seem overly simplistic, the fact is that people spend a lot of their time putting thought and energy into routine tasks day in and day out. These are the 80 percent tasks in the 80/20 equation. By putting in place a simple checklist to remind people of these tasks, they are freed up to focus their minds and their energies on the more important jobs at hand. A good checklist is the key to actually implementing any SOPs.

12. UTILIZE THE ELITE WEEKLY PRODUCTIVITY TRACKER

This is a tool that helps team members look at their day, their week, their month, and their quarter all on one dashboard so that they can locate all of their top priorities in one place. Discussed more fully in chapter 10, the Elite Weekly Productivity Tracker is one of the most useful tools offered in the Elite Execution System.

13. HAVE CLEAR ALIGNMENT

When you have clear alignment with yourself, you are focused on your day-to-day activities, on your long-term goals, and on making sure that you are spending your time building the habits that are going to get you to where you want to go. When you have clear alignment with your team and your leader, you are all on the same page regarding what your individual priorities are and how they fit within the goals of the organization.

14. BUILD YOUR GRIT

What the 20-Mile March is to organizations, grit is to individuals. Grit is the great differentiator, the secret weapon that separates the greatest, most successful people in the world from everybody else.

Grit author Angela Duckworth defines the term this way: "Enthusiasm is common and endurance is rare. Grit is passion and perseverance towards long-term goals."

In other words, don't confuse grit with drive and passion or even skill. Lots of entrepreneurs are very driven and motivated and will put tons of energy and time into their businesses, working seventy, eighty, even ninety hours a week. They will have tremendous passion toward a goal for a short time. But when the excitement and the newness of constant change get replaced with the mundane aspects of execution, their excitement and energy wane. They look for greener pastures and something else to put their energy and passion and drive into. These people lack grit.

When it comes to developing grit, it helps to keep this formula in mind: Effort times talent equals skill. Skill times effort equals results. Effort counts twice.

15. BE OBSESSED AND HUNGRY

Actor Will Smith summed up what it means to be obsessed and hungry perfectly when he said, "The only thing that I see that is distinctly different about me is I'm not afraid to die on a treadmill. I will not be outworked, period. You might have more talent than me, you might be smarter than me, you might be sexier than me...But if we get on the treadmill together, there's two things: you're getting off first, or I'm going to die."

It is really that simple. The person who is willing to hustle the most and outwork the competition is going to be the person on top.

16. BUILD HABITS AND DO THE ACTIVITIES THAT DRIVE RESULTS

Discipline is giving up what you want right now—short-term happiness and short-term gratification—for what you really want, which is achievement and fulfillment.

Really productive people understand that although you need discipline to build a habit, once that habit is in place, you can focus your mind and your energy on improving another aspect of your life or work. It's a chain reaction that begins with building habits through discipline and ends with driving the results you are after.

17. TRACK YOUR PROGRESS

As Peter Drucker said, "What gets measured gets improved."

This sums up the importance of tracking your progress. There are many ways to do that, and in the Elite Execution System, we use a number of tools ranging from scoreboards to a Living Fully Dashboard, to the Elite Weekly Productivity Organizer, to the Elite Journal. Journaling can be one of the most effective ways to build habits and achieve incredible results.

18. PROSPECT AND SELL

It is everybody's job to prospect and sell. Everyone in the organization is responsible for driving revenue, not just the sales team. In fact, every interaction with a client, vendor, or partner is an opportunity to prospect and sell. If everyone— from accounting to HR to legal to operations—takes on the responsibility of driving revenue through prospecting and selling, it's going to drive a tremendous increase in productivity. Everyone should feel it is their job to help the company find new opportunities and *sell* the solutions we provide to potential clients and customers. This simple shift in attitude makes a dramatic difference in our ability to drive revenue, which, at the end of the day, is productivity.

19. STAY ON YOUR 20-MILE MARCH

Each team member is responsible for maintaining a 20-Mile March mindset and following their own 20-Mile March best practices.

This includes meeting the commitments that they make to their team, tracking their progress with each individual and team goal, and using the 20-Mile March tools referenced throughout this book. It also entails doing more of the 20 percent of activities and disciplines that will drive consistent results.

20. TAKE MASSIVE CONSISTENT ACTION

Contrary to what a lot of so-called business gurus will tell you, people succeed by doing more, not less. Nobody gets to the top of their game taking shortcuts. They get to the top by doing more of the activities that drive results, and less of the unproductive activities that do not. You must take that 20 percent of your most productive activities and double or triple your time and efforts in relation to those activities. Do much more of the right things, and your business will see exponential growth.

In the next few chapters, I will expand on the value of adopting the use of Rocks, WIGs, and several of the other productivity and execution tools referred to in this roadmap. I encourage you to download the entire 20-Mile March Roadmap to Success document from the DLP Elite website, DLPElite.com, and adapt it to your own organization.

CHAPTER SEVEN

ROCKS

Would you like to accomplish more in just ninety days than your competitors accomplish all year? If you are building an Elite Organization, the answer is obviously yes. Through Rocks, that is exactly what you will do.

A Rock is a solid commitment to achieve a particular outcome in a defined amount of time. Rocks are your top priorities for the next ninety days that, when accomplished, will move you toward achieving your One-Year Bull's-Eye, your Three-Year Aim, your BHAG, and your mission. Before you adopt the discipline of Rocks, it is important to understand what they are *not*.

First, don't fall victim to the trap of enthusiastically setting a bunch of really great-sounding goals and calling them Rocks. Rocks are not pie-in-the-sky aspirations or all the dreams you have for the future. Do not approach Rocks with the attitude that "it would be really great if I could get this done next quarter" or "it would really help us if I got this or that done by year's end."

If you consistently miss your Rocks—the inevitable result of reaching too far or being too vague with your short-term goals—you end up causing your team members to lose confidence in you and your business, which is precisely the opposite effect that Rocks are intended to produce.

Second, keep in mind that Rocks are not the responsibilities you already have or the activities that you already engage in on a day-to-day basis. They are not the unanticipated issues that inevitably crop up or the intermittent fires that you have to put out simply by virtue of being in business. Rocks are part of a strategic plan. They are the specific, measurable, attainable, relevant, and timely (SMART) goals that you choose to make your biggest priorities for the next ninety days.

Each team member in your organization will have three professional Rocks and three personal Rocks each quarter. I will give you a simple example of how to go about setting Rocks through the most common type of personal Rock people choose: weight loss. If you wanted to lose weight, you might define your Rock as "I am going to eat better and lose weight." That is not a Rock, though, as it is not SMART. It is not specific and cannot be measured. There is no accountability to achieving the goal as you cannot clearly track if you reached it or not. If you "ate better" but gained weight, did you accomplish the goal? If you lost two pounds, did you achieve the Rock?

A SMART Rock related to weight loss would be, "I am going to lose fifteen pounds this quarter." This is specific, measurable, attainable (presumably, depending on how much weight you have to lose, your metabolism, etc.), relevant, and timely. This is how all Rocks have to be set. They must be SMART.

I will give you another example. Recently, a new property manager at one of DLP's rental communities wanted to improve rent collections. The community she was managing had higher than targeted delinquent rent, and this was the biggest challenge in the community achieving its budget. In her first attempt at setting a Rock, she said, "I am going to get better at collecting rent." This is not a Rock, though, as it is not SMART. There is no way to determine or measure its success.

Now, if she said she was committed to "reducing delinquency by 2 percent by the end of the quarter," that would be a SMART goal—that is, a Rock (assuming a 2 percent reduction is attainable at this community). This Rock is specific, measurable, relevant, and timely; at the end of the quarter, she can look at her collections and know whether delinquency was lowered by 2 percent or not.

ROCKS ARE UNIVERSAL AND PERSONAL

At DLP, we establish six Rocks a quarter for the overall organization, followed by six Rocks for each team or division.

If you are like DLP and have multiple business units, you will also want to establish Rocks for each business unit and each division or team within those units. At DLP, we have six Rocks for our lending business, six Rocks for our real estate brokerage business, and six Rocks for our construction management unit, and so forth. In addition, as we have grown, each function area—including marketing, accounting, IT, legal, and HR—has begun establishing its own set of Rocks.

For example, a Rock for the real estate brokerage business,

DLP Realty, might be to increase residential real estate listings by 10 percent. DLP Realty's marketing team might set a Rock of increasing inbound marketing leads by 20 percent.

Each individual team member will have three professional Rocks that will often be in support of the team's Rocks. In the DLP Realty example, therefore, an individual member of the marketing team might set a Rock of increasing their number of social media posts promoting DLP Realty by 50 percent.

Each team member will also have three personal Rocks that have no direct relationship to furthering the goals of the company. The weight loss example mentioned previously is a typical personal Rock. A personal Rock I have established for myself for the current quarter is to have at least twenty-one outdoor activities with my family.

It's very important to note that each Rock has just one owner; Rocks are never shared. So regardless of whether it's a personal Rock, a team Rock, or an overall organizational Rock, one individual owns that Rock; and that one person takes responsibility for achieving that particular Rock. The team member who owns a team or company Rock counts that Rock as one of their professional rocks. So, as an example, if you are the head of sales and you own the top organization Rock of "achieving X number of sales," that would be one of your three professional Rocks.

MANAGING ROCKS WITH MILESTONES

Think of Rocks as your ninety-day world. It can become very easy to get off track toward achieving a Rock without even realizing it. To stay on track, you are going to need a checklist of sorts, and that is where milestones come into play.

Milestones are the building blocks of Rocks. They are the achievements that you need to accomplish incrementally within the ninety-day period in order to complete the Rock. Milestones are tracked every two weeks. Your first milestone would be due fifteen days into the quarter, your second milestone in thirty days, your third milestone in forty-five days, and so forth. You end up with six milestones per Rock, with the final milestone being what has to be achieved in order for the Rock to have been accomplished.

The following provides an example of how you, as a DLP team member, would determine a Rock.

Let's say you're a service (maintenance) supervisor at a four-hundred-unit apartment community and one of your key responsibilities is getting vacated apartments ready for the next resident. Your company goal is to achieve five-day unit turns, which means that when a resident moves out, the vacated unit will be ready to reoccupy within five days. In the industry, this is often referred to as the time it takes to "make ready."

Your current make ready rate is ten days. As the service supervisor, you know that reducing this timeframe is a huge priority and one of your biggest performance drivers. At the end of Q2, June 30, you establish a Rock to bring the make ready average in this apartment community down to five days by September 30, the end of Q3.

You're now going to break that Rock down into milestones. One of the best ways to set up milestones is to alternate between activity-based and results-based milestones.

Milestone one, your first activity-based goal, will be to assess the capabilities of your current vendors and staff—including flooring installer, painters, and cleaners, to name a few—and use what you learn to build a new turnover plan. You set July 15 as the deadline for this milestone. The new plan you develop to complete milestone one will lay out specific steps on how to reduce turnover from ten days to five days by the end of Q3.

Milestone two, a results-driven goal, will be to get the turnover average down to eight days. You commit to do this by July 30. Milestone three is to implement pre-move-out inspections where you'll be assessing, before the resident vacates the apartment, what work will be needed to turn over the unit. This system, which will be implemented by August 15, will help you get materials ordered and vendors lined up.

Milestone four is to bring the make ready average down to six days by the end of August. Milestone five will be to evaluate and tweak, as needed, the new make ready plan by September 15. And by the time you reach milestone six, which is to get your make ready average down to five days by September 30, you will have accomplished your Rock.

Of course, as the service supervisor, you did not meet these milestones and accomplish this Rock on your own. You needed the support and help of your team—in this example, your three service technicians who report to you.

One of those technicians could own the job of getting each apartment cleaned out—disposing of any leftover resident items, pulling out carpet, demoing damaged kitchen countertops, and so on—so the vendors who need to do the turnover work can get started.

If you have any chance of getting to your five-day unit turn-over Rock, this service technician is going to need to speed up the clean-out process. How will he accomplish this? By setting his own Rocks and milestones, which will play out something like this:

Service technician's Rock: Achieve a one-day prep and clean-out average by September 30.

Milestones to achieve this Rock:

→ Milestone one: Clearly measure average unit clean-out time over the first two weeks.
→ Milestone two: Implement a clean-out checklist.
→ Milestone three: Conduct pre-move-out inspections using the pre-move-out inspection form.
→ Milestone four: Complete move-outs for the month on average in three days.
→ Milestone five: Conduct pre-move-out inspections at least five days before move-out.
→ Milestone six: Complete all September post-move clean-outs in one day.

By following this schedule and meeting his milestones, this technician will meet his Rock. If, for some reason, he falls behind on a milestone mid-Rock, he has time to realign and pivot, reset priorities, or rethink processes. As long as every-one in the company has set Rocks and milestones like this service technician and his supervisors, the company will steadily make progress toward completing its most import-ant goals.

MILESTONE TO BHAG

It is easy to get bogged down in the execution details of Rocks and milestones and lose sight of how they fit into the overall strategic picture.

All the milestones that each individual accomplishes every couple of weeks lead to achieving their Rocks, which, in turn, contribute to the company meeting its overall top Rocks. Quarter after quarter, these Rocks build up until, at the end of the year, the company meets its One-Year Bull's-Eye. Then, in three years, the Rocks will have helped the company meet three years' worth of bull's-eyes so that it can meet its Three-Year Aim. Hitting bull's-eyes year after year will make it possible to truly live your purpose, achieve your mission, and accomplish your Big Hairy Audacious Goals (BHAGs). By adopting the discipline of Rocks throughout your company, I can almost guarantee that you will get more done in ninety days than your competitors get done in a year or more. Rocks provide the competitive edge so you can blow past your competition and achieve incredible results in a shorter timeframe than most would think possible.

HOW TO IMPLEMENT ROCKS

Working in a system of milestones and Rocks requires a certain rhythm, a definite cadence. This is where the discipline of Rock setting comes in.

DEFINING ROCKS

Every quarter, as part of the Elite Execution System, the company defines its Rocks. This is a very open and transparent process that typically begins about thirty days before the end of each quarter, when you start thinking about your biggest priorities for the next quarter. This is also when you start organizing your Rocks.

At DLP, we call this process the three sixes, since each team has six Rocks, each individual has six Rocks—three professional (remember a company or team Rock counts as an individual's professional Rock) and three personal—and there are six milestones to meet (one every two weeks) for each Rock.

The first step in establishing the discipline is getting the team committed to doing this—driving it as a focus and a priority—weeks out before the start of the next quarter. In order to reinforce its importance, setting Rocks should be brought up in nearly every meeting and be a part of nearly every internal company communication. This is the time to remind all team members that their Rocks must be set before the beginning of the quarter and that they must meet the SMART criteria. You must take time to train and teach your team how to go about choosing and defining Rocks.

Choosing Rocks can be difficult for some team members. I recommend that business unit leaders hold a clarity session with the team a few weeks before the beginning of each quarter to collectively develop a good list of potential Rocks, followed by an active and open discussion to determine the team's six top priorities. Once those priorities are established and Rock owners are designated, the rest of the team can consider what Rocks they can establish in furtherance of these goals.

I highly encourage you to build a routine where the Friday before the end of any quarter, leaders present their company or team Rocks, as well as each of their own and their team members' individual professional and personal Rocks, to the executive team in a live presentation. This allows the senior leaders of the organization to review the Rocks, help refine them, ensure they are SMART, and reinforce the company's commitment to accountability.

At DLP, we do this every quarter, and I personally am a part of all Rock presentations, providing engaged, supportive, and critical feedback as needed. We are pros at Rocks at this point and know that they are incredibly important to the continued success of the organization. Being this involved with Rocks reviews may seem like a lot, but I know it is a great use of my time and the time of all my leaders.

ROCKS IN PROGRESS

The team leaders are responsible for keeping track of Rocks, and that begins with assessing where each person is with respect to their milestones every two weeks. These regular check-ins help individuals track their own achievements as they either mark their milestones as complete (and their Rock on track) or as not accomplished (marking their Rock as off track). This process continues through the quarter, allowing team members to pivot as necessary to get off-track Rocks back on track whenever possible.

Since implementing this system around eight years ago, DLP team members have improved consistently and are now accomplishing approximately 90 percent of their Rocks—up from the 50 percent we were lucky to achieve in the beginning—which has driven the company's very consistent and profitable growth year after year. Creating and sustaining a discipline of Rocks can seem daunting, but I can assure you that once this becomes a regular rhythm in your organization and you start accomplishing your biggest priorities quarter after quarter, you'll get buy-in throughout the organization. Every tool you need to start implementing the discipline of Rocks in your organization will be covered in chapter 9, "Communications and Meetings, and chapter 10, "Organizing and Productivity."

But before we get to those topics, I want to share with you how to achieve your biggest and most important goals—through the commitment of a team—that will move your organization forward at speeds you have only, up to now, imagined.

CHAPTER EIGHT

WIGS

WILDLY IMPORTANT GOALS

In the last chapter, I told you about how incorporating Rocks into your organization's operating system will help each team member individually grow, stretch, and achieve professional and personal goals faster than they ever thought possible. Now I am going to introduce the practice of WIGs—Wildly Important Goals—which will propel your company on a path of accelerated growth.

Where Rocks are owned by individuals, WIGs are owned by teams.

The WIGs concept was first introduced by Sean Covey in his book *The 4 Disciplines of Execution*. The four disciplines Covey presented in the book are:

→ Discipline one: Focus on the wildly important.
→ Discipline two: Act on the lead measures.
→ Discipline three: Keep a compelling scoreboard.
→ Discipline four: Create a cadence of accountability.

Before I walk through each of these disciplines in detail and explain how they fit into the Elite Execution System's Operations Quadrant, I want to share an epiphany I had when I first became aware of the WIGs concept.

THE ISSUE WITH EXECUTION

Every person in a position of responsibility in every fast-growth company in the world has an issue with being reactive; and being reactive interferes with execution.

The faster and bigger a company grows, the more often unanticipated matters rear their heads. These constant fires, these never-ending whirlwinds of time-stealing urgency, interfere with everyone's ability to execute.

When you do manage to put out a fire or two long enough to actually move forward proactively on executing an important goal, you are hit again, before long, with a new tsunami of urgent matters that pull you back into reactive mode. It's a cycle that business owners and their leadership team repeat over and over. This scenario is the biggest impediment to execution; and when you stop executing, you stop growing. We can call this the whirlwind.

The epiphany I had a number of years back is this: the urgent things are usually not that important.

That feels counterintuitive. When you are faced with completing a transaction, or solidifying a deal, or addressing an issue that is happening in real time, you feel in that moment like it is the most important thing in the world. But the reality is that urgent priorities—the whirlwind—are rarely what is most important. In addition, what IS most important is rarely urgent.

Another way to think about this is, the urgent priorities act upon you, whereas the most important priorities are those you must act upon. This is what makes focusing on what is most important so hard; it must be proactive versus all the reactive urgent priorities that come at us each day. If you are going to go out and execute on the tasks that you must do to meet your WIGs, you need to put in place a discipline and routine that allows this to happen. You need to step out of the demands of the here and now for a relatively small amount of time so that you can focus on what is wildly important. This isn't some mystical approach to avoiding having all of those urgent priorities and fires that we all have to deal with each day in a rapidly growing company. I'm not offering you a magic wand to make them all disappear. There are always going to be urgent priorities that need your attention, and sometimes they will come at you faster and heavier than other times. The implementation of WIGs will, however, make sure you are still accomplishing your biggest and most important goals that will lead to consistent and incredible growth—despite the whirlwind—to execute on the matters that promote long-term, consistent, and exponential growth.

DISCIPLINE ONE: FOCUS ON THE WILDLY IMPORTANT

The first discipline of execution is to focus on the wildly important. This discipline requires that you take the time to figure out what really drives results.

Ask yourself: What is the one goal that, if met, would make most of your other goals irrelevant? This becomes your WIG.

It is possible that you already know what your WIG should be. But it is more likely that you have so many big priorities and goals that choosing just one presents a challenge. Perhaps you spend so much time dealing with urgent matters that the concept of choosing one priority goal seems overwhelming.

If you aren't sure what your WIG should be, I recommend you sit down with your team and make a list of all of the important priorities you want to achieve. Take that list and isolate the two or three most critical priorities that would make the biggest impact on achieving your vision. Then ask yourself which priority matters more than any other. Which priority, if achieved, would catapult your organization forward more than any other? Put that one at the top of your list. It is your WIG.

The next question to ask is if everyone on the team will have a role in achieving this goal. If the answer is no, then you may want to either reconsider prioritizing this WIG or choosing a second WIG that the team members who cannot impact your first WIG could impact. You might even make this second WIG a sub-WIG—a smaller priority—that will play a significant part in achieving the primary WIG.

Keep in mind that a WIG is achieved through the team's efforts, so it is crucial that every person on a WIG team has a role in moving metrics and a real impact in achieving the WIG. As you go through this process, remember that there will always be more good ideas than the capacity to execute. You are going to have to prioritize goals. This quote from Apple CEO Tim Cook has helped me think through priorities when setting goals:

[Apple is] the most focused company that I know of, or have

ever read of, or have any knowledge of. We say no to good ideas every day. We say no to great ideas in order to keep the amount of things we focus on very small in number so that we can put enormous energy behind the ones we do choose.

Apple has tens of thousands of team members and they're doing forty billion dollars a year in revenue. Their successful business model—one worth emulating—is to put enormous energy behind a very few great ideas.

Once you determine your WIG, you need to set parameters for achieving it. Start by identifying where you are, where you want to be, and when you want to be there. In other words, define a starting line, a finish line, and a deadline. All WIGS must have a finish line in the form of from x to y by when.

For example, last year we set a WIG for our People or HR department to fill twenty open seats with Rock Star A Players over a four-month period. We phrased this as, *Our WIG is to "go from twenty open rock star seats to zero open rock star seats by April 30."* Zero open rock star positions becomes our lag—or end goal—measurement.

DISCIPLINE TWO: ACT ON THE LEAD MEASURES

The second discipline to achieving your WIGs is acting on the lead measures.

Lead measures are the actionable leverage points that you control in order to achieve your end goal. A great quote by Archimedes that illustrates how useful leverage points are is, "Give me a lever long enough and a fulcrum on which to place it, and I shall move the world."

Like Archimedes's lever, lead measures are all about being able to achieve a really big goal by focusing on moving the point of leverage. In other words, the lead measures are the actionable things you can do today in order to influence the achievement of your lag or result measurements, the things that tell you whether you accomplished your WIG.

Implementing lead measures must heighten the probability of achieving the WIG. Let's say, for example, you have a goal of losing twenty-five pounds—going from 175 to 150 pounds—in three months. Weighing 150 pounds is your lag measure. The way to achieve that goal is to burn more calories each day than you consume. So two lead measures to lose twenty-five pounds in three months might be to (1) consume less than 1,500 calories each day and (2) to exercise enough to burn 2,500 calories each day. The lead measures are the means of getting to your end goal or lag measure. We often focus too much on our lag measurement—losing twenty-five pounds—without considering how we'll get there. No one can lose twenty-five pounds by simply thinking about it or wishing it, but you *can* control how many calories you consume and burn. If you focused on managing these measurements—what calories you consume and what you burn—you'll be able to lose that weight. (I bet you did not expect you would learn the secret to weight loss when you bought this book, did you? In all seriousness, hopefully this simple illustration has convinced you about the importance of lead measurements.)

There is no exact right number of lead measurements for the achievement of a WIG, but a good range to target is four to eight.

When you first set up your WIG, it is vital to determine who participates in achieving that particular goal. The primary criterion is that each participant must be able to influence at least one lead measurement. There's no right or wrong number of people who should be part of a WIG, although we usually settle on anywhere between six and twelve people in order to keep oversight and accountability manageable.

Returning to the DLP WIG of filling twenty key Rock Star A Player seats, the team undertook a number of lead measures, or influencing activities, to bring us to our desired result. These included posting job ads, prospecting potential candidates, conducting first interviews, and taking part in panel interviews.

DISCIPLINE THREE: KEEP A COMPELLING SCOREBOARD

The third discipline of achieving your WIGs is to keep a compelling scoreboard. This discipline is based on the principle that people play or work much harder when score is being kept.

People like to win. It motivates them. If some neighborhood kids are out playing pickup basketball and you are watching them play, it is very easy to tell if they are keeping score or not. The level of intensity, focus, energy, and effort goes up tremendously when score is being kept. People just play differently when you keep score.

This same mindset happens in business. Without a way to keep score, people don't know if they're making progress or not, if they are doing well, or if they are doing poorly. They don't know if they're achieving the goal or falling short. And even worse, they stop caring. They become disengaged.

To be effective, your WIG scoreboard must be designed and controlled by the players themselves. The scoreboard should be highly visible, compelling, and simple to follow. It must reflect accurate lead and lag measures, as well as each WIG team member's score. When looking at the dashboard or the whiteboard or the poster board—whatever the team constructs the scoreboard to be—each team member should know exactly where they stand and where each of the other team members stands. It should be easy to see if they are winning or not.

You can find examples of compelling player scoreboards on the Elite website at DLPElite.com.

DISCIPLINE FOUR: CREATE A CADENCE OF ACCOUNTABILITY

Discipline four, create a cadence of accountability, is the discipline of execution. It is all about holding the team accountable to executing on the lead measures that will accomplish your WIG.

The center of this discipline is the WIG session, a short weekly meeting where each team member reports on their success or failure in meeting the commitments they made during the previous week's meeting. The WIG session is held on the same day and time each week and nothing other than the achievement of the WIG is mentioned during the meeting. The entire focus of this meeting is accountability for moving lead measures forward.

Ideally, the WIG meeting is led by a rising leader, someone you're grooming to grow into a position of greater responsibility and leadership.

The WIG leader starts off the meeting by succinctly stating the WIG, what progress has been made to date, and whether the group is on track with the WIG. Then, beginning with the leader, each team member tells the group the commitments they made the previous week, the results of those commitments, the lead measures that they moved the past week, any lag measures achieved, and whether they are winning with regard to their goals. The individual reporting ends with the actual words, "Yes, I am winning," or "No, I am not winning." Then the next team member gets up and does their report.

After all the team members finish reporting on their results, the leader recaps all of the lead and lag measures and then makes two or three commitments for what they will accomplish in the coming week. Each team member follows suit, making two to three new commitments, and then the leader adjourns the meeting.

Applying this cadence to those twenty Rock Star A Players we were looking to hire at DLP, a typical meeting around that WIG would go something like this.

Kate, the leader of this WIG, would start off the meeting by saying, "Our WIG is to go from twenty open rock star seats to zero open rock star seats positions by April 30. My commitments this week were to, first, complete three interviews and make two decisions on two key leadership candidates and, second, to review all open key seats and finalize roles with the recruiter. The results of the commitments are that all interviews were complete; drafted career success offers were completed pending final feedback from executives; the key seat review meeting with a recruiter was complete; I conducted two first interviews, one second interview, and completed two career success offers. Right now, there are six key leader open seats, and in total so far, we've hired fourteen producers, and yes, I am winning."

Jason, our chief of staff, would be up next. "My commitments last week were to get two career success offers out to candidates and to complete new job ads for all open positions. My results are: I actually sent out three career success offers. I posted one new job ad for the only open position I currently have. I had two prospecting calls. I put two candidates into screening. I had four first interviews and three panel interviews. No career success offers have been sent out yet this week, and right now I have three seats that are open, and so far, I've hired two Rock Star A Players. Yes, I am winning."

The next person goes until everyone reports their results. Then we each take turns setting our two or three commitments for the next week. This entire process typically takes less than twenty minutes.

When we set the WIG of twenty seats filled, it sounded like an unbelievable number to meet. I'm happy to report that this awesome team succeeded in filling the twenty seats with Rock Star A Players in less than the four months we set for the deadline of the WIG. I have no doubt that if we did not have this WIG, there's no way we would have filled even half of the seats we were after.

Along with the benefits of reaching the goal, an equally exciting benefit of WIGs concerns the alignment and relationships that get built when team members hold each other accountable. Meeting consistently every week and working together to achieve big goals is a really powerful and tremendous team-building tool.

WINNING WIGS

Unlike Rocks, which must be accomplished in ninety days, there is no time limit for WIGs. I have been a part of WIGs that are less than three months and WIGS that have taken nearly one year. In my experience, the four- to six-month timeline works best, but it really depends on the nature of the goal.

It's very rare for a team member to achieve 100 percent of their commitments every week. The team will decide what constitutes winning or losing. Typically, that number will hover around 80 percent. Sometimes teams agree to let each member determine what winning means for themselves. The percentage isn't important; what matters is that there is an established and consistent method of accountability and that you are moving toward achieving your WIGs.

If people are consistently missing their commitments, it is up to the leader of that WIG to hold them accountable. When I am WIG leader, I might suggest to the person who is falling short that we follow up offline and talk about how I can be of assistance in getting them back on track. It is critical that each team member contributes their part to winning the WIG. If a team member is not carrying their weight, a decision will have to be made about whether the team member is simply not doing their part, is not clear on what they can do, or is, at the end of the day, the wrong person to be a part of this WIG.

If the relevant team is not making solid progress in achieving the WIG, I encourage you to undertake a problem-solving session—something we call an IDS that is covered in detail in the next chapter—to determine what needs to happen to get the WIG on track. Sometimes, the WIG itself needs to be reconsidered. Maybe it is no longer the WIG of the team.

Maybe the right people are not participating in the WIG, or perhaps the team is just too caught up in the day-to-day whirlwind and needs to regroup, refocus, and be reminded of why this was established as a WIG in the first place.

Regardless of your industry or the size and maturity of your business, implementing WIGs can absolutely transform your organization, but you have to make sure that you adopt the communication tools that support all of your goals being fully implemented throughout your organization.

CHAPTER NINE

COMMUNICATIONS AND MEETINGS

Meetings can be the most efficient and effective way to foster great communications throughout a company.

Unfortunately, in many organizations, meetings are viewed as a waste of time or as a distraction from getting real work done.

I have talked to many executives and leaders in different types of industries, and before they implemented the Elite Execution System, most were convinced that meetings were the enemy. Almost universally, these leaders saw a benefit in having fewer meetings, not more.

They were not entirely wrong. In many organizations, meetings really are a waste of time and absolutely worthy of a high performer's disdain. I'm hopeful, however, that after reading this chapter you will be converted into accepting that, when done properly, meetings can be the most productive time of your day and week. All I ask is that you proceed with an open mind, because almost every aspect of the Elite Execution System hinges on developing a great meetings rhythm throughout your organization.

THE CASE FOR MORE MEETINGS

When a company is just getting started, when there are three or five or maybe ten people total on staff, communicating isn't that complicated. Everybody probably works in the same location and can just walk (or yell) down the hall when they need something. It is easy for people to get together to talk through issues and discuss opportunities. There is no need to be formal about it.

But as companies grow, and divisions or teams are created, people are no longer so easy to access. You can't just turn around and talk to a colleague on the spur of the moment. It becomes impossible for every stakeholder to be a part of every relevant conversation without some kind of planning and structure.

As this growth takes off, things start falling through the cracks. We start relying on what seems like an endless number of emails to communicate updates, discuss issues, or attempt to put out fires, often with few tangible results. Supervisors become frustrated because their reports aren't fulfilling obligations. Team members are unsure about their responsibilities and what expectations are, let alone how to be accountable for meeting those expectations. Lack of communication leads to confusion, missed opportunities, and even stagnated growth.

It is no wonder that the biggest complaint that most team members have in high-growth companies is a lack of communication. Unintentional as it may be, keeping team members in the dark damages morale, fosters confusion, and results in higher rates of disengagement and turnover.

If your business is fast growing, you will soon start to feel the effects of these breakdowns in communications, if you haven't already.

The good news is that once you do establish a great meetings rhythm, it will serve as a centering force for your organization, building consistency within your ranks as team members start to understand priorities and how to hold each other accountable for execution and results. This will lead to better engagement, improved productivity, and increased profits.

DAILY AND WEEKLY MEETINGS RHYTHM

Under the Elite Execution System, each team member should expect to attend a minimum of nine internal recurring meetings a week. For senior leaders, that number will generally be higher, possibly as many as fifteen prescheduled recurring meetings each week.

I know that sounds like a lot, but if you follow this meeting rhythm, you will realize it takes a lot less time than you would expect and will actually save you time by helping you solve issues and make decisions much faster.

The weekly meeting rhythm consists of five daily huddles, one Level 10 Meeting™, one WIG session, and two pipeline meetings. Together, all of these meetings should take up a maximum of three hours of your time each week. The amount of productivity and actions this will drive in just three hours of time per week is tremendous and will have a huge impact on setting and keeping your company on a high-growth and high-profit path forward. Let's look at each type of meeting.

THE DAILY HUDDLE

The rhythm of the daily huddle is simple. As the name suggests, these occur every day, and every team member participates in one. I recommend holding huddles first thing in the morning to help people get into a good mindset for the day and to get their energies going. The exact time you choose doesn't matter as long as you stick to the same time each day. Choose a time that works best with the start time of your team members.

There is no set rule about who belongs in what huddle. You can do it by division or by team. People can participate in person in the office or, if they work remotely, via Zoom. Huddles can have just four or five people or as many as twenty, although in my experience, eight to fifteen people per huddle tends to be the sweet spot.

The purpose of the huddle is to quickly run through what is going on with each person. The simple format is that each person takes a turn reporting on their two key numbers, their successes, what they are focused on today, and what they might be stuck on.

Let me walk you through a daily huddle through the example of a typical DLP salesperson's huddle report, which will highlight the two most productive tasks that a salesperson engages in—meetings and calls:

> My successes are Dominic invested $100,000, Darrel invested $300,000, and I received a referral from one of our team mem-

bers, Josh. On the personal front, my Rockets won last night. My first metric is I had one meeting yesterday and I had twenty-three calls. Today, I'm really focused on bringing in commitments from the event last week, and I'm not stuck on anything today.

The next person, a coordinator on the same team whose job is processing investor paperwork, might say:

My successes were that we brought in a little over a million dollars in new wire transfers yesterday. Yesterday, I had two IRAs move forward through processing, and finalized three signatures for non-IRAs. What I'm focused on today is training a new assistant, and I'm stuck on receiving the accreditation proof from Randy's attorney.

One of the most powerful aspects of the daily huddle is for team members to be able to tout their successes and for their supervisor and fellow team members to recognize their accomplishments. Daily encouragement goes a long way to build teams and drive engagement and productivity.

In addition, the huddle gives the team member a chance to ask for help if they are stuck on something, as it may be a problem the supervisor or another team member can easily solve. In the example above, for instance, the sales coordinator is stuck on paperwork from an investor's attorney; the salesperson may be able to resolve that quickly with a call to the client. The huddle also gives supervisors the opportunity to intervene if a team member does not seem to be spending their energy on what is most important to the team or the company. It gives team members a forum in which to engage with their teammates and to communicate with their leader. It allows a leader the opportunity to recognize if a team member is struggling personally or professionally by focusing on not only the information they are reporting but their level of engagement and energy as well.

When I first implemented the daily huddle in my company over five years ago, many of my executives pushed back, telling me this was a terrible idea. Their arguments were that they talk to their people enough and they couldn't see any value in something so repetitive and structured. Now the consensus among almost everyone is that the daily huddle is the most important meeting in their entire day and that they could not imagine not having it as a daily staple.

LEVEL 10 MEETINGS

Level 10 Meetings are one of the most critical tools in the Elite Execution System. I learned Level 10 Meetings from the great Gino Wickman, author of *Traction*. The goal of the Level 10 Meeting is to get each team to operate at peak performance, at the highest level, which is at level ten.

Although we usually run our Level 10 Meetings weekly, some teams hold them biweekly or even monthly, depending on their needs or structure. For our purposes here, however, I'm going to talk about Level 10 Meetings as an important weekly discipline.

These meetings follow a set format: report on successes, review key numbers and scorecards, review Rocks, update or share news and headlines, and review the to-do lists from previous meetings. Each of these sections should take no more than five minutes. The final part of the Level 10 Meeting—and also the most robust and critical—is when you dive into actually solving issues. We call this IDS—Identify, Discuss, and Solve. This may run forty-five minutes to an hour or more. The following is an explanation for how each part of the meeting works.

Report on Successes

Every Level 10 Meeting starts off upbeat, with individual team members sharing about their successes. This is a great way to get people engaged, especially the team members who tend to remain fairly quiet in meetings. You probably have noticed that the same people are always eager to answer questions or give their opinions in meetings, while others sit back and are hesitant to chime in.

Focusing on success first gives the supervisor a chance to acknowledge certain people who are doing a great job but aren't extroverted enough to speak up on their own initiative. The more people you can get talking in the meeting, the more attentive, focused, and engaged everyone becomes. Often, the quietest folks have the most to offer. Encouraging them to speak up about their successes is a great way to encourage them to participate in other areas as well. I recommend having every person in the meeting share at least one personal and one professional success from the past week.

Review Key Numbers and Scoreboards

Whether you keep track of your key numbers using scoreboards, scorecards, or some other form of tracking, this is the time to let everyone know how the team is performing as a whole with respect to your set business goals. The format is flexible as long as you allow each team to see whether they are on or off track with their goals. If the team is off track, you want to identify that as early as possible so you can begin addressing the issue to get back on track.

Review Rocks

Next, each team member reviews the team Rocks that they own for that quarter and reports on the status of each. If a milestone is due, they report whether they have accomplished that milestone or not. If all is going well, they mark their Rock as on track. If they are behind, they mark their Rock as off track. As will be discussed later, off-track Rocks become the subject of further discussion during the issue-solving portion of the meeting.

News and Headlines

The news and headlines update is an opportunity for the leader and others to share whatever is going on in the organization or with individuals that might be of common interest to the group. This might include company news such as new hires or awards, team member accomplishments, or any type of personal news that anyone wants to share. It is also a time to remind staff of upcoming meetings, events, and deadlines.

Review To-Dos

In this section of the meeting, the team takes a look at the to-do lists that were created in previous meetings. Each individual reports on the status of the to-dos assigned to them, marking them complete when they are done, and discussing the status of any outstanding to-dos. If the to-do is not accomplished, it may lead to an issue-solving discussion. When new tasks are assigned in the issue-solving section of the meeting, which we cover next, they must be added to the to-do list to provide accountability regarding the completion of the task.

Issue Solving with IDS

This last section of the Level 10 Meeting is devoted to issue solving. The method used is called IDS, which, as mentioned earlier, stands for Identify, Discuss, and Solve.

This is an opportunity for each team member to bring forward any issues they are grappling with, including any off-track Rocks, so that they can tap into the power of the team to find a way to solve them.

Sometimes there are only a handful of issues to bring forward, and other times there are dozens of issues brought forward in just a single meeting. It is up to the leader to prioritize the issues, so it is possible that not every issue will get covered during the meeting. But as long as the group has the opportunity to tackle the most important matters, the rest can wait for the next meeting or be resolved through another avenue.

Here is how a typical IDS session works.

First, the leader reviews the list of issues brought forward and prioritizes the top three, always starting with the most important. He or she does not move to the second most important issue until the first issue is solved. In some meetings, you may solve only one issue, and in others you could end up solving many. Regardless, you can consider your IDS meeting to be a success as long as you focus on your most important issue first. The team member who brought the issue forward should lead the discussion around it.

What is really interesting and beneficial about this process is that the issue raised by the team member is not always the issue that needs resolving. Often, what is frustrating them is a mere symptom of a larger issue. The IDS process is an excellent way to get to the bottom of what is really going on. Because so many people are looking at the problem from all angles, the likelihood increases that the collective mind of the group will identify the root issues.

For example, a team member might say, "I need more help because I'm spending all my time dealing with customer complaints." In their mind, the issue is too many customer complaints to be handled by available staff, and a proposed solution is to hire more help.

But in the IDS session, the team will dig deeper, asking questions about what the complaints are about and why there are so many in the first place. Is there a problem with the product that is being sold? Is it being oversold? Is the real problem with another internal process? As the team dives into the issue, they may discover the real problem is that customers have a *reason* to complain—there is an underlying issue with the product. By getting to the root of the actual problem, the team is able to address its cause, solving the problem at its core. This IDS approach not only saved the company the additional cost of hiring another team member, but it also saved the company untold amounts by fixing a problem that could have cost the organization customers and damaged its reputation.

Once you embrace this process and start conducting regular

Level 10 Meetings, you are going to be amazed at how many issues you can actually solve in a weekly sixty- or ninety-minute meeting. So often, the things that nag and frustrate team members can be resolved very easily. Sometimes all it takes is for somebody to make a decision or to take action; sometimes all that is needed is for someone to empower that team member. And sometimes, like the customer service situation discussed above, the problem can only be solved when you get to the real root of the matter.

We have a tool—discussed in detail in the next chapter—that helps teams get to the root of the problem, and in turn its solution, much faster. We call it the Elite Executive IDS Summary. This tool can lead to significant breakthroughs; it helps a team member holistically analyze an issue and lay it out in a format that allows the rest of the team to clearly understand the problem. In addition, the tool forces the team member to think through a proposed solution, including the pros, cons, costs, and action steps needed to implement it.

The Elite Executive IDS Summary is available for download on the DLP Elite website at DLPElite.com.

TYPES OF LEVEL 10 MEETINGS

When your company is still fairly small, you will probably want to conduct a single Level 10 Meeting for everyone involved in your business. As your organization grows, however, it is going to make sense to branch out into specific Level 10 Meetings for different areas of your business. At DLP, we have a weekly Level 10 Meeting for each business unit or division. In addition, we have Level 10 Meetings for different focuses, such as "shared function" meetings that we do less frequently, perhaps on a biweekly or monthly recurring schedule.

For instance, at DLP, we run a biweekly HR Level 10 Meeting with just the members of that department and the business unit leaders. In that meeting, we focus exclusively on matters connected with hiring, developing, and retaining great people. We also have a monthly Delivering Wow Level 10 Meeting led by our chief experience officer who is joined by leaders and frontline team members from each business unit. We have a monthly IT Level 10 Meeting with our IT team and the business unit leaders that is narrowly focused on IT issues. However you decide to organize your own meetings, it is very important to keep them structured and consistent.

WIG SESSIONS

The third type of core organizational meeting is the Wildly Important Goal (WIG) meeting, which we covered extensively in chapter 8. The twenty-minute WIG meeting should be set on a regular weekly timetable, and its sole focus should be on achieving that specific WIG. Only the team members involved with that WIG should attend.

PIPELINE MEETINGS

The final type of recurring core meeting is the pipeline meeting. Conducted twice a week, pipeline meetings can be great revenue drivers that significantly reduce turn times, regardless of what type of business you are in.

The idea is to keep your pipeline—whatever that is and however it works in your business—moving forward. It is about holding each team member accountable for their piece of the process. When people know they're going to have to report on the status of something or someone moving through a pipeline, it forces them to up their game. Not only are they going to be held to a higher level of personal accountability, but being in a pipeline meeting helps them understand how important their role is in achieving the goal. It helps each person see how they are an important part of a much larger process.

As with the Level 10 Meetings, the composition of the pipeline meeting will follow the growth of your organization. If your business is relatively small, everybody in your organization will be in the same pipeline meeting twice a week. As your business gets bigger, people will likely break out into different pipeline meetings, covering just the portion of the process they are involved with.

If I were running the HR department of a business, for example, I might have a pipeline meeting about moving candidates from screening through hiring. If I were in lending, I would have a pipeline meeting about moving people from applying for a loan through closing on that loan. And if I were in real estate brokerage, I'd be having a pipeline meeting about people going from that first appointment with an agent through buying or selling a home.

Whatever service you're providing or product you're producing, the pipeline meeting is designed to help smooth out the process from beginning to end.

For a pipeline meeting to be as effective as possible, you need to have a pipeline tracker. This is a place where you can see the status of the widget as it moves through the pipeline—

for example, moving the client, loan, or potential new team member through the process from x to y. This is best done using your core business operating system, such as your construction management system, property management system, CRM, investor management system, ATS, or any other workflow/operating system that you use to run your business. If you do not have that system today, then a pipeline can be managed in an Excel document or Google sheet. We have operated many of our teams' pipelines from Google sheets over the years.

The DLP Elite website is full of templates and tools to help organize and run your own organizational meetings.

ALIGNMENT MEETINGS

It has been said that people join companies and they leave bosses. I believe this to be true the vast majority of the time.

Often, people are so busy and embroiled in so much day-to-day communication on projects, fighting fires, meetings, and simply dealing with the whirlwind that there is very little time for real alignment and connection between a leader and their report. Even if you sit right next to your report every day and talk all day, it is critical that you take the time to step out of the whirlwind and focus on your report at least once per month. This is the time where you build relationships and trust, establish accountability, and get aligned with the responsibilities and expectations for the team member, areas of improvement needed, and opportunities to grow and develop to achieve personal goals and fulfillment.

These monthly alignment meetings are arguably the most

important of all of the forms of meetings in the Elite Execution System.

In the next chapter, I will be introducing the Elite Alignment Workbook, which is an amazing tool that will help you create and maintain a structure to establishing alignment. Here, I discuss the goals of the Elite Execution System's alignment and the best practices we have found for establishing an alignment meetings rhythm.

GOALS OF ALIGNMENT

Most high-growth organizations consistently struggle with accountability and alignment. You are going to have a hard time growing profitably without clear ownership or accountability and alignment between leaders and their reports.

The goals of the alignment meetings are to drive accountability and build relationships that will make this accountability—and simply dealing with the day-to-day work challenges—easier and more enjoyable. Keeping alignment as a priority will help people stick with your company, their role, or a project or priority even when things are hard, they're frustrated, and everything is not going the way they want. Alignment meetings done with passion and genuine care build loyalty and engagement and will drive significant increase in productivity and results.

ALIGNMENT MEETINGS RHYTHM

Under the Elite Execution System's alignment meetings rhythm, you will have a total of twelve meetings each year, or one meeting per month consisting of eight monthly huddles, two full alignment meetings, and two performance evaluations.

Monthly Alignment Huddles

The format of an alignment huddle is pretty simple. In this one-on-one meeting with their supervisor, the team member shares their personal and professional successes and reports on any to-dos they had on their list from the previous alignment huddle.

The team member shares their IDS topics, which can be any professional or personal issues they want to address, big or small. This entire meeting will generally be around thirty minutes.

From your perspective as a leader, the more your team member shares about their personal lives, the better. You want to build a deep relationship where your team member is comfortable sharing personal information with you. As a leader, you should know a good amount about the life of each of your reports.

ARE YOU INVESTING ENOUGH IN YOUR REPORTS?

Here is a simple test to determine if you are investing enough in your reports. Can you answer at least eight out of these ten questions for each of your reports? If you can't, you need to work on getting to know your reports better.

1. Married? If yes, what is their spouse's name?
2. Have kids? If yes, how many? Names? Ages?
3. How many siblings?
4. Parents alive?
5. Where did he or she grow up?
6. Favorite sports team?
7. Hobbies or passions?
8. Pets?
9. Own a home or rent?
10. Faith an important part of life?

Full Alignment Meetings

The format for the full alignment meeting is the same for the alignment huddle, with the addition of a deeper dive into the Elite Alignment Workbook, discussed in chapter 10. During this meeting, you and your report will go through the entire Elite Alignment Workbook, focusing on the team member's development plan, understanding their big goals and aspirations as well as the immediate goals and challenges. This meeting, which is conducted at least twice per year, should take ninety minutes to two hours in addition to the time spent reviewing and updating the alignment report prior to the meeting.

Performance Evaluations

During the twice-yearly performance evaluations, the discussion should focus on the team member's performance, their development plan, and performance goals. It is the leader's job to provide open and candid feedback on where the team member is falling short and areas where improvements are needed, along with a review of responsibilities and expectations. It is critical that leaders give clear, direct, and specific feedback on areas of needed improvement, in addition to making sure to highlight how the team member has improved or any of their great accomplishments since the last performance evaluation. This meeting will take ninety minutes to two hours, in addition to a similar amount of time by both the team member and the leader to prepare for the meeting and complete the evaluation.

The Elite Alignment Workbook, which includes each meeting template plus DLP's performance evaluation template, is built into the proprietary technology and available at DLPElite.com/Tools.

ADDITIONAL RECOMMENDED MEETINGS

All of the meetings discussed above are critical staples of the Elite Execution System. Each of the additional meetings that I will cover, although not required as part of the operating system, are highly recommended.

DRIVEN FOR GREATNESS

Driven for Greatness is, in short, a book club. Driven for Greatness is also one of our core values, and it means "seeking knowledge." Many of our team members say this meeting has been truly life changing. This is a voluntary meeting that we do at 8:00 a.m. on a Thursday every other week. We provide each team member with a corporate Audible account, and each team member downloads the book and listens to it on their own time, often during their drives to and from work. We have two discussions a month around each book, each led by a different team member.

The preference is for a frontline team member to lead the discussions. It's a great opportunity for people who are really focused on growth, learning, and knowledge seeking to be surrounded by other people who have similar interests. It's also a way for team members who are on different sides of the company and who would otherwise never see or talk to each other to build close friendships. Outside of the biweekly meeting, members meet with each other one-on-one on the alternate weeks to build relationships and help each other grow. The books we read are chosen by the members based on a survey we send out, which is made up of recommendations by members. We read books across topics such as leadership, personal development, habit building, and goal setting. Driven for Greatness has been tremendously powerful for over a decade now; we have read well over a hundred books as a group since we started.

ALL-COMPANY TEAM MEETING

We do a company team meeting every month. This is a sort of rah-rah-type meeting where we talk about all the company's successes and all the personal successes people are having in their lives.

At this meeting, we announce a core value of the month, and we talk about how we're doing with achieving our BHAG and where we are with our PPP.

Each of our function leaders gives an update on what's going on in their teams. We also talk about important company-wide initiatives and trainings. We announce a team player and sales professional of the month every month, highlight all of our new team members, and announce birthdays and anniversaries since starting at DLP. This meeting provides great energy, excitement, and transparency throughout the organization.

MONTHLY LEADERSHIP MEETING

We run a monthly leadership meeting for anyone who is either in a supervisory role or has the potential and desire to move into a leadership role. The sole focus of this meeting is developing leadership skills, knowledge, and abilities. We mix up the content between trainings, issue solving, coaching, and other forms of development. We also read leadership books a few times a year.

WEEKLY EXECUTIVE MEETING

In our weekly executive meeting, I take the opportunity to make sure I'm providing clear communication to my executive team, while also giving them the opportunity to bring forward issues they need to discuss with me. This meeting provides a clear format and method for the executive team to communicate our critical overall priorities with each other and to also determine how to communicate these priorities throughout the company. We follow the Level 10 Meeting format for this meeting.

RULES FOR MEETINGS

In order to maximize the usefulness of meetings, we have developed eleven rules to increase engagement and lead to better communications, decisions, and results. The first seven apply to all meeting types, and the final four apply to Level 10 Meetings.

1. Every meeting must have a clearly defined leader who runs the meeting and the screen, keeps the team on track, and leads the IDS discussion. In addition, we have a secretary or meeting recorder who takes notes, records the meeting, and makes the to-do assignments.
2. The leader must send out a meeting reminder with an agenda the day before meeting.
3. All members are to report on their personal and professional successes.
4. Video must be for all members, via Zoom.
5. Everyone must bring *energy* to every meeting.
6. All members are expected to come to each meeting fully prepared.
7. The leader must send a recap email after each meeting.
8. All Level 10 Meetings must follow the Level 10 format in its entirety.
9. All Level 10 Meetings must include a review of Rocks and turn anything off track into IDS topics.
10. All Level 10 Meetings must utilize the Executive IDS Summary to tackle IDS topics.
11. At the conclusion of every Level 10 Meeting, each member is required to rate the meeting on a scale of one to ten.

QUARTERLY CLARITY SESSIONS

Every quarter, we conduct a focused clarity session that can last anywhere from five to ten hours. Although this is a big commitment of time for me and other company leaders, it is well worth it as the results have been tremendous.

We conduct a clarity session for our parent company each quarter and one for each business unit. At these sessions, we make sure we are aligned with our compass, review our current quarter performance, and prepare for our next quarter, including setting our next quarter's Rocks.

We spend most of our time—as much as three or four hours—during the clarity sessions solving issues. We often spend two or more hours setting the next quarter's Rocks and we spend generally around thirty minutes to an hour reviewing our performance on the relevant quarter's Rocks, and undergoing the IDS process for any Rocks that were missed.

The last significant part of the clarity session is usually spent on people. Because the number one driver or restriction to achieving a clear plan is almost always people, we take the time to discuss our C players and how we plan to resolve our people issues. We spend time discussing our open seats and roles we are hiring for, as well as how to develop our high-potential team members.

Strategy Session 1

In addition to our quarterly clarity session, we conduct two strategy sessions per year, which we call Strategy Session 1 and 2.

Our first quarterly meeting is Strategy 1 and occurs in December or early January of each year. This is the time that we lay out our updated Elite Compass for the next year, draft our One-Year Bull's-Eye and Three-Year Aim, and write our annual strategy statement. We review our core values, our purpose, mission, and BHAG and clearly set out the state of the organization and our direction forward. We set the next quarter's Rocks and determine our people, acceleration, and operations plans for the next year. We spend significant time at these sessions solving issues.

A typical one-day strategy session meeting agenda would be:

8:00 A.M.	MEPS and Key Questions
8:30 A.M.	The Compass Draft
10:30 A.M.	Budget Review
11:00 A.M.	Key Numbers Review
11:30 A.M.	People Plan
1:00 P.M.	Operations Plan: Rocks and WIGs
2:00 P.M.	IDS
4:00 P.M.	Acceleration Plan
5:00 P.M.	To-Do Recaps

If possible, I recommend turning the Strategy 1 session into an executive retreat. We typically start Friday, meet all day, and then do a dinner out together. Saturday, we start early, usually with some sort of group activity such as kayaking, basketball, or biking. Then we meet all day Saturday as well. This gives us more time to dive deep into IDS sessions, and often we end up having eight to ten focused IDS sessions. As we have grown, we have broken out into smaller groups for IDS sessions as well. Saturday night, we usually do some sort of party/night out. Often, we finish up Sunday with breakfast and a few last meetings.

We begin the meeting with a MEPS session where we go around the room and each team member reports, in one sentence, on how they feel mentally (M), emotionally (E), physically (P), and spiritually (S). At the end of their statement, each person says, "Checked in."

This MEPS check-in process—something I learned from Young Presidents Organizations—helps each person focus. The idea is to acknowledge and then let go of any stressful or tired feelings so participants can give all of their attention to the meeting.

After the MEPS session, each team member goes around the room answering a few key questions. We mix these questions up, but typically, we ask team members things such as, *What should we start? What should we stop? What should we keep doing?*

Next, we move into a deep discussion about the compass, followed by a detailed review and revision of the budget. We then review our key numbers, look at where we currently stand, and talk about what our goals are for the next year.

After that, we move into discussing our people plan for the new year, which includes a discussion about any C players, a review of empty seats, and a discussion about high-potential team members. We then talk about operations or execution with a focus on Rocks and WIGs, move into IDS—a topic that, if we let it, could comprise the entire meeting—and follow that up with a discussion about our acceleration plan for the new year. We wrap up by reviewing to-dos that were assigned during the meeting, making sure every task is owned and has a due date.

Strategy Session 2

Around midyear, we meet for Strategy 2 meeting. Strategy 2 is essentially a hybrid of the Strategy 1 meeting and the clarity sessions. We spend more time reviewing the compass than in a clarity session and discuss how our direction may have changed from the start of the year, and then devise an updated strategy statement and compass if needed.

We also take a deep inventory of where we are off track or have fallen short in achieving our One-Year Bull's-Eye, and we let that drive our Q3 Rocks, our WIGs, and our people discussions. We generally turn this into a weekend retreat as well, similar to Strategy 1 session.

Who Should Participate

It is important that you have the right people in these sessions. I recommend including your key leaders—the people who drive your day-to-day results.

Detailed downloadable information to help you create your own quarterly clarity and strategy sessions can be found at DLPElite.com.

COMPANY DAYS

Each year, we operate five all-day DLP Days, which are attended by everyone in the company. The five days are Vision Day, Issue-Solving Day, Alignment Day, Living Fully Day, and Frontline Obsession Day.

We make all five of our DLP Days a really big deal. We get everyone together first thing in the morning for a company-wide huddle. We run a company presentation in the morning, and we provide lunch to everyone. We require everyone to wear DLP clothes, and we take lots of pictures, which we share during our presentation and via a social feed so we can all see each in real time, despite being in different locations. We want to keep everyone excited, pumped, and energized.

One of the ways we get our team members to engage at this high-energy level is that we invite our team members to participate in planning the days by asking them questions such as, *What has been your biggest accomplishment this past year? What will be your biggest accomplishment this year? What is the number one opportunity for us to improve on?* During the DLP Days themselves, we break into interactive workshops that involve personal sharing and problem solving.

Vision Day

Vision Day is held in January of each year. Its purpose is to share the direction and vision of the organization with the entire company. We lay out our compass and One-Year Bull's-Eye for the new year, share our strategy statement, and get the whole company excited about the journey and the march we are about to set out on. We also tell our story of how we got where we are to date.

Vision Day is an interactive event. It begins with all of our team members taking individual or group pictures wearing their company gear and posting to a shared social media feed. Since we have team members all over the country, this helps us all see each other, and it helps everyone get energized and excited about being a part of one team. Then we present the compass and strategy statement of our parent company, DLP

Real Estate Capital. We do so via a PowerPoint presentation, with videos streamed via a live Zoom feed to all of our offices. After the company-wide presentation, our teams break out into the individual brands or business units and cover the Elite Compass for their specific companies.

Next, we engage everyone in a fun and interactive session where each team member answers questions such as, *What will be your two biggest accomplishments this year and why? What have been the three most impactful events in your life so far? What can DLP do to help you achieve your biggest goals?*

These prompts get everyone talking about how we can go out and execute and what we need to do to improve every aspect of our business. This important process gets everybody engaged, communicating not just to leaders but also to each person in the organization. Helping each team member understand how they fit in is incredibly powerful in starting the year off right and in getting everybody moving and executing in the same direction.

Make sure you record your Vision Day. It makes for an excellent recruiting tool throughout the year and should be part of the onboarding process for all team members who join you. Watching a recording of your last Vision Day helps new team members understand the mission of your organization, as well as how they can impact results and contribute to achieving your purpose.

Issue-Solving Day

In April, we hold Issue-Solving Day. The purpose of this day is to address the biggest issues that team members have identified and shared to date. We break out into preset groups so we can tackle issues in the order of importance, as determined by the group.

The idea behind Issue-Solving Day is to tackle as many problems as we can for a full day in order to clear the path for our teams to move forward. It's incredibly powerful and enlightening for the leaders and for the team. We use the Executive IDS Summary—which can be found at DLPElite.com—for all issue presentations.

Alignment Day

We hold Alignment Day—a full day focused exclusively on providing team members and their leaders with the opportunity to get realigned with each other—in July.

The importance of this day cannot be overemphasized. We start out in the morning with a company-wide meeting and training on alignment, and then team members and their reports break out into one-on-one alignment meetings designed to help them get back on track so they can really focus on building their relationships.

Living Fully Day

We hold the fourth DLP Day—Living Fully Day—in October.

As the name suggests, this is a really fun day where we focus on just about everything other than work. We start the day off with an optional 5:00 a.m. club workout and an 8:20 a.m. prayer. Living Fully Day is a jam-packed day of fun, positive energy, and excitement.

Along with the early morning workout, team members are invited to participate in all types of physical activities—from yoga to dancing to priming to CrossFit—and we have team members present life-enhancement sessions on topics such as personal finance, sleep, stress management, priority management, and parenting.

We also include a project that is designed to give back to those in need or who serve our country. Last year, we offered team members the opportunity to participate in hand-writing cards to deployed military.

Frontline Obsession Day

This DLP Day is a little different—it is all about our senior leaders spending time directly with the front line, working alongside them in the field. Our senior leaders choose what roles they are going to do and then coordinate to spend time doing tasks such as construction, maintenance, leasing, answering the phone, or doing coordinator-type tasks. This exposure to seeing what we are doing directly in the front line gives our leaders tremendous perspective. It is also meaningful for frontline team members to see DLP leaders roll up their sleeves and do work alongside them.

COMPANY PARTIES

In addition to all the meetings and company days previously discussed, we make sure to do at least two or three company get-togethers a year. We have found that holding regular company outings—holiday parties, picnics, volunteering with a nonprofit, or just a happy hour on a Friday—where we can get team members engaged really helps maintain relationships between team members. These outings are especially great for keeping team members who don't work on the same teams engaged. At DLP, our staples are our annual summer picnics and Christmas parties.

CHAPTER TEN

ELITE ORGANIZATION AND PRODUCTIVITY

People who work in high-growth companies constantly feel like they are caught up in a whirlwind of nonstop emails, phone calls, and meetings. Is it any wonder that they lose focus and their minds become scattered as they try their best to process the never-ending feeds of information?

Even though people are putting in longer and longer hours, the majority of their time is still spent on matters that do little to directly further the mission of the organization. More time at work does not usually equal greater productivity. Team members lose sight of the fact that 20 percent of effort drives 80 percent of productivity, as we discussed in chapter 6. They are spending more time at work while accomplishing less, and all at the expense of their home and spiritual lives.

So many people feel burned out, dissatisfied, and disengaged at work and in life that the paradigm has to shift; and with the Elite Execution System, it does.

The first shift in changing this cycle must occur at the organizational level. As a business leader, you must embrace the concept of Living Fully and accept the fact that team members who feel they are making enough time for all of their priorities—what we call the 8 Fs: faith, family, fitness, friends, finance, freedom, fun, fulfillment—are going to be *more* productive at work, even if that means they end up working fewer hours. Our goal here is to foster what we call work-life integration, where each team member, by integrating all areas of their life, is able to simultaneously make progress and achieve personal life goals while still progressing in their career. In order to become an Elite Organization, you must embrace and champion your team members living full lives.

Before getting into how to foster this full life and goal-achieving feeling in your team members, I want to acknowledge a fact. The average American spends over two hours per day on social media and nearly four hours per day watching television. Everyone has the same amount of time. Most people are not actually overworked and most do not have a time management problem; instead, they have a priority-management and a lack-of-discipline problem.

In order to drive priority management and discipline so team members can be productive and happy, team members require three types of alignment:

First, alignment with themselves. This means aligning what they want to accomplish in life with where they are today, how they spend their time, and what changes they need to make to achieve their goals.

Second, alignment with their leader. Team members must be

aligned with their leader on what the priorities are, how the team member is performing, and what needs to happen for the team member and the leader to achieve their goals.

Third, alignment with their team. Team members must be aligned with their teammates on the priorities, focus, and direction of the team.

The Elite Execution System offers team members tools to achieve alignment. The primary tool is the Elite Alignment Workbook, which is a Google sheet. Alternatively, the Elite Alignment Workbook and all the rest of the Elite Tools are built into the proprietary technology built for the Elite Execution System, available at DLPElite.com/Tools. Within the Elite Alignment Workbook, there are a few tools built in. The main tools are:

→ A Life Designing and Goal Setting tool that allows team members to assess various aspects of their lives, followed by a framework so they can set and achieve meaningful goals
→ The Living Fully dashboard
→ One-page personal plan
→ The performance evaluation

In addition, there are a number of other critical elite tools outside of the Elite Alignment Workbook, including:

→ Elite Weekly Productivity Organizer
→ Elite Journal
→ Elite Leadership Toolbox
→ Elite Executive IDS Summary
→ DLPEdge.com

The key for all of these tools to be utilized and to truly drive alignment is the one-on-one alignment meeting schedule between the leader and the team member, discussed in chapter 9.

At DLP, we also offer the opportunity to join support groups, including prayer groups, fitness challenges, a 5:00 a.m. club, and a moms group. In addition, we provide external tools such as Audible, Fitbits, and Beachbody on Demand.

As we walk through each of these methods and tools, you are invited to download more information about them, as well as the actual workbooks and templates referenced, from DLPElite.com.

ELITE ALIGNMENT WORKBOOK

The Elite Alignment Workbook is an incredibly powerful workbook with a range of tools that focus exclusively on the team member, helping them align with their short-term and long-term goals, as well as with their leader and team. I will walk you through each tool in the Elite Alignment Workbook.

LIFE DESIGNING AND GOAL SETTING (LIVING FULLY DASHBOARD)

Every DLP team member participates in Life Designing and Goal Setting at least once per year. This elite exercise guides each team member through an assessment of all areas of their life so that they can set goals that allow them to take control of their time, while designing a life that will make them truly happy, fulfilled, and prosperous. We call this the 8 Fs of life: faith, family, friends, finance, fitness, freedom, fun, and fulfillment.

If you are a leader who is thinking, "I need my people putting all their time into their work; I don't want them distracted and working less," you are not alone. Many leaders feel this way. But the reality is that encouraging your team members to put all their focus and energy into working eighty hours a week might benefit your organization in the short term, but sooner or later, each team member's lack of fulfillment in other areas of their life will bleed into work, causing all kinds of problems. You will start seeing an increase in health issues—including heart-related and other physical ailments—mental illness, substance abuse problems, and other effects of burnout, such as absenteeism, decreased productivity, a toxic work environment, team members experiencing personal relationship problems, and losing great people who will naturally want to seek out a better working environment.

This is why you must focus on helping your people live a full life that integrates work with all of their other priorities that make up the 8 Fs of Living Fully—faith, family, fitness, friends, finance, freedom, fun, and fulfillment.

The Life Designing and Goal Setting exercise requires team members to assess their lives across all of the 8 Fs simply by scoring themselves across a range of questions from one to five. After they complete the assessment, they will see their Living Fully wheel-of-life hat, which will visually show them where they are in need of improvement. Team members are then encouraged to list out their goals—both big and small, and as many as they can think of—for each area of their lives. Then, after brainstorming and daydreaming about their goals for each of the areas, team members are asked to prioritize their top ten or so goals for the following twelve months, taking care to focus on each of the 8 Fs, especially the ones in need of significant improvement. This top ten list for the following year is another tool within the Elite Alignment Workbook called the Living Fully dashboard and is a simple way to evaluate how well you are performing against the top goals you set for the year.

The Life Assessment and Goal Setting tool, along with the Living Fully dashboard, encourages each team member to take control of their life and to realize that you can have it all. Real success comes from achieving fulfillment in all of the areas of your life that are important to you, not just a few. Sometimes people who are great at work neglect family time or personal finances or their fitness/health. Eventually, those neglected areas will catch up with them and affect other areas of their life, including work. When we give team members the tools and resources to assess and improve on every aspect of their lives, we find that not only do they become happier, healthier, and more engaged in their lives in immeasurable ways, but the organization also benefits in terms of that team member's increased productivity.

ONE-PAGE PERSONAL PLAN

Next in the Elite Alignment Workbook is a one-sheet document called the One-Page Personal Plan. This is a really critical tool to help team members connect the dots between their big goals and how they spend their time, which is what will ultimately dictate if they achieve their big goals. The tool begins with the team member listing their long-term (ten- to twenty-five-year) aspirations or goals. Then they put down their one-year activities that will drive them to achieve those aspirations and the ninety-day actions they must take.

Next, the team member lists out their strengths, their weaknesses, and the big opportunities where they think they could drive their 10X results. This is followed by a section called "My 20 Percent," where they list what they feel should be their 20 percent most productive focus and narrow that down to their 4 percent most productive focus (the 20 percent of 20 percent previously discussed) so that they can isolate and concentrate on their most productive tasks.

The last, but arguably most important, section is called "Priority Management." This section is about determining habits to start, stop, or keep doing. We list out some examples—going to bed early, rising early, reading, education improvement, personal time, exercise, and diet, to name a few—to help them think through what new habits might help add to their success. Then the team member lays out a schedule that accounts for the activities and actions they must take to achieve their goals set for the quarter and the year and that will move them toward achieving their long-term aspirations.

This is where the rubber meets the road. The majority of people who set goals never significantly adjust how they actually spend their time; and in order to get different results, a person must change. They need to incorporate habits and routines that will move them toward their goals and away from past lackluster results. This requires not only adding new habits but also breaking old ones. The one thing we cannot create is more time. So when you add something new to your schedule, you must remove something else.

Creating a schedule that has time allocated to move team members toward each of their top ten goals and that allocates time to help them improve their performance in the workplace is a really powerful—and simple—exercise. It merely requires laying out an ideal weekly schedule starting from when they want to wake up to when they want to go to bed. It's important to block in time for the obligations that cannot be currently changed, as well as time for the activities they will need to engage in to achieve each of their goals. They will also need to plan for any unscheduled activities that could pop up, as well as reactionary tasks such as email and returning calls. Care needs to be taken to focus on those 20 percent most productive activities, as well as provide for enough time to achieve each of their top ten goals for the year.

Once each team member is confident that they have a schedule that is realistic and will move them toward their goals, then it is about putting that schedule into action. This requires adjustments in routines, updating any currently used calendars (such as Google calendar), and then constantly monitoring and adjusting the schedule as needed.

ALIGNMENT HUDDLE AND ALIGNMENT MEETING TEMPLATES

Within the Elite Alignment Workbook are templates for the alignment huddle and meetings we discussed in chapter 9. For each month's meeting, you simply copy the template and rename it "Current Month Year Huddle or Meeting." It is the team member's job to fill out the monthly meeting tab and lead the discussion.

PERFORMANCE EVALUATION

The last template in the workbook is the team member's actual performance evaluation template. Using this template, the team member responds to each question with a self-rating of

A, B, C, or D. In addition, the team member comments about their performance in each section of the evaluation and adds a self-assessment of their overall performance. There is also a detailed development plan template included so that the team member and the leader can together develop strategies to help the team member drive A-level performance in their current role, and outline the next step in their development path.

Based on their self-ratings of each question, the team member will receive a score of their overall performance and a total grade: A, B, C, or D. After the team member completes the self-evaluation, the leader then completes their evaluation of the team member. All of this is completed before the live performance evaluation discussion.

We recommend creating a new tab for each performance evaluation and keeping them all in the same workbook for each reference to reflect back and evaluate growth and progression.

ELITE ALIGNMENT WORKBOOK RESPONSIBILITIES

Each team member has five jobs related to the alignment workbook. They are expected to:

1. Invest the time to fill out the alignment workbook fully
2. Keep the alignment workbook up to date
3. Fully prepare for the alignment meetings
4. Remain open and vulnerable
5. Make sure the alignment meeting is held every month

It is the responsibility of the leader to:

1. Review the alignment workbook fully

2. Coach and support team members
3. Show genuine care and interest
4. Provide accountability and clear direction
5. Make sure the alignment meeting is held every month

You will notice that it is the responsibility of both the leader and the team member to make sure the meeting is conducted every month. This is because it can be very easy to fall out of rhythm and stop doing alignment meetings, sometimes for months. It is especially tempting to skip them when you are really busy.

Do not skip them.

Over the long term, conducting alignment meetings will save you tremendous time. If you are struggling to dedicate an average of one hour per month for a direct report—for a person who is spending forty or fifty or more hours per week working for your team—then you need to reevaluate your priorities because, as I have emphasized throughout this book, your people are your greatest priority. The only way you can achieve incredible results month over month and year over year is through great people who are fully engaged, aligned, and accountable. In short, invest the time.

ELITE ALIGNMENT WORKBOOK SHARING

There is one last aspect of this powerful tool I want to discuss, and this is the importance of sharing the contents of the Elite Alignment Workbook.

It bears reemphasizing how important this is: the more team members are willing to share and have open discussion about all areas of their lives, the better. As a leader, you want to build open and full relationships with your reports, which leads us to a second aspect of sharing. I recommend that leaders also share their alignment workbooks with their reports. The more open you are with your reports and the more they feel they know you, the more open and vulnerable they will be with you as their leader.

I share my Elite Alignment Workbook with the entire DLP organization. This accomplishes several things. First, the fact that I fully use the tool and keep it up to date shows that I walk the walk and really believe in the tool. Second, it helps my team get to know me better and, in turn, builds trust. And third, it serves as an example of how to fully and properly use the tool.

ELITE WEEKLY PRODUCTIVITY ORGANIZER

The Elite Weekly Productivity Organizer is another simple tool to help team members keep themselves on track on a daily and weekly basis. The endless emails, calls, urgent priorities, requests, and tasks that we all face each day—that never-ending whirlwind—can leave each of us feel overwhelmed. The Elite Weekly Productivity Organizer keeps all your top priorities—Rocks, WIGs, and your key numbers—front and center and helps you focus on making progress toward your top priorities each day despite the whirlwind. The organizer also helps you track and organize your daily and weekly world by tracking your daily huddle successes, top focuses, and what you are stuck on, as well as your weekly commitments and to-dos in your WIG sessions and Level 10 Meetings.

Each daily huddle team should have a master productivity

organizer with each team member having their own tab for their organizer. You can find the Elite Weekly Productivity Organizer template on DLPElite.com.

ELITE JOURNALS

If you have never used a journal before, my guess is the idea of journaling is going to sound silly to you and you may discount it as a waste of time. The truth is, daily journaling not only increases productivity but can also help reduce stress, benefiting each team member and the organization as a whole.

Elite Journals are quarterly journals where you first lay out each of your six quarterly Rocks and your habit-building focuses. You begin each day journaling what you are grateful for and your personal BHAG that you want to accomplish—an incredibly powerful habit—in addition to your top three goals or priorities for the day.

Then you write out your schedule for the day. Throughout the day, you take notes or jot down thoughts and ideas. There is a section where you can list any of the day's wins or accomplishments, as well as a section called What I Learned Today. Finally, there is a second Attitude of Gratitude section—filled out at the end of the day—where you list what made you particularly grateful on that day.

There are also spaces to list out any metrics you are tracking or habits you are building. You can report on your number of steps, your workout results, the book you are reading, the amount of sleep you had, calories consumed and/or burned, meditation results, or just about any other data you are focusing on tracking and improving.

I resisted the idea of journaling for years and years, but I have now become an avid journaler and a believer. I have both experienced firsthand and witnessed in others how powerful a consistent journaling practice can be to help you stay focused, achieve your goals, and put yourself in a grateful mindset at the beginning and end of each day.

Elite Journals can be purchased on DLPElite.com.

LEADERSHIP TOOLBOX

A leadership toolbox is a place where you organize leadership resources. This can be a simple Google Drive or Dropbox folder or simply a Google sheet where you have easy access to your leadership resources.

At DLP, our leadership toolbox includes a list of our favorite leadership books, past leadership training links, our definition of leadership, and the job of a leader. In short, it is a library of resources to become a better leader.

DLP EDGE

DLP Edge is DLP's learning system. Edge stands for Where Education Drives Greatness in Execution.DLPEdge.com is a learning platform, with hundreds of trainings and university-style curricula (such as Sales University). I highly recommend investing the time to build a real learning platform like DLPEdge.com. It takes time and commitment, but the dividends are incredible.

Our system was built on the thinkific.com platform, and we are in the process of expanding it such that fellow Elite Execution System implementers can plug into it. Depending on when you read this book, this may already be live and will be accessible on DLPElite.com.

ELITE EXECUTIVE IDS SUMMARY

The Elite Executive IDS Summary is an excellent tool to help individuals and teams solve their biggest issues and maximize IDS sessions. If, like many leaders, you find that your meetings are ineffective and important issues are not getting resolved, it is likely that you can look to three main reasons:

→ The person bringing the issue forward does not clearly articulate the issue, resulting in confusion among team members. For example, a typical complaint is "We need to communicate better." Although this is undoubtedly a true statement, there is more going on here than just a failure to communicate. Often, communication failures are signals or symptoms of much larger issues that need to be addressed.

→ There are no proposed solutions or action items. People can provide insight, feedback, and engagement much more easily and effectively when there is a proposal for a solution on the table.

→ People often hold meetings as a replacement for doing the hard work of thinking. I see this a lot—an issue that did not actually need to be addressed in a meeting or discussed in the context of a meeting now taking up the time of five or ten people talking it through. It could have been resolved if just one person had spent the necessary time and energy to figure out a solution.

The Elite Executive IDS Summary solves all three of these

issues. It allows a team member to fully think an issue through, clearly lay out possible solutions, propose adoption of one of the solutions, and then lay out action items to implement the proposed solution. The team member can also address the pros and challenges of each solution, as well the cost and timeline for implementing the solution.

Using the Elite Executive IDS Summary can be incredibly clarifying. In our experience, it allows the team member to not only figure out their own solution but also to lay out their own clear path to implement the solution.

In all the other cases when the team member still needs the input of the rest of the team to solve the issue, the act of laying out the issue and proposing a solution encourages engaged and productive conversation, allowing the team the ability to get to the best solution and action plan much more efficiently. The column to the right of the presenter's inputs is where members participating in the discussion can provide their feedback.

Sometimes this feedback will help confirm the proposed solution, allowing the team member who proposed it to get buy-in; other times the proposed solution and plan will be very different than what is finally decided.

The Elite Executive IDS Summary, and all of the other tools discussed throughout this chapter, are all built into the proprietary Elite Execution System technology, available at DLPElite. com/Tools.

Next, we are going to talk about how to accelerate the growth of your business.

CHAPTER ELEVEN

ELITE ACCELERATION

Elite Acceleration is all about creating a clear plan to generating revenue that will propel your growth and allow you to achieve all of your goals.

Acceleration involves marketing and sales working together to serve your core clients and customers, while differentiating your organization from the crowd of competitors.

Most organizations treat marketing and sales as two completely different functions. Executives direct their marketing teams to create brochures and other collaterals, build websites, produce content to drive social media traffic, and develop different types of campaigns to generate leads. They direct their sales staff, meanwhile, to prospect, conduct sales appointments, and close sales. This failure to integrate sales and marketing, along with a lack of clear understanding of who their core clients are and how to differentiate their products or offerings from the competition, creates serious barriers to acceleration.

In today's economy, driving acceleration can be confusing,

overwhelming, and frustrating. There are more options for marketing and advertising than ever before; there is also more competition for the attention of buyers than ever before. This leads many leaders to the conclusion that their efforts are expensive and ineffective.

The way to combat all of this is to have a clear acceleration plan. A plan that helps you look at sales and marketing as one, and gives you the framework to focus on the key components that will generate accelerated revenue, including a clear lead-generation plan and an expert position content plan that not only lets you tell great stories to show how your product solves the problems that your target or core clients are facing but that also follows a formula for presenting that product in a way that is different from your competition. Through an Elite Acceleration Plan, you will generate and convert more leads, resulting in closing more sales and retaining more clients.

Before we dive into the details of how to accomplish Elite Acceleration, I want to explore the concept of acceleration a bit by introducing the concept of the flywheel.

THE FLYWHEEL

What fundamentally drives your business? Who are your best clients? What do they really want? What do your products offer that is different from what the competition is offering?

Answering these questions begins with understanding the key components of your business that make up your flywheel.

The concept of the flywheel was introduced by Jim Collins

in his book *Good to Great* and further discussed in his book *Turning the Flywheel*.

If you have ever been fishing, you are familiar with the feeling when you first get a bite and start cranking that fishing reel. It feels like it is sticking at first as you slowly, deliberately turn that crank with increased effort, turning it again and again and again until by the eighth or ninth turn, you have got that reel spinning almost on its own power and you are reeling that fish in. The circular mechanism that produces that spin, the flywheel, can generate tremendous momentum after the investment of significant and consistent energy or action to turn the wheel.

Companies are often looking for the one big thing that can drive their revenue and growth. But the reality is, like the flywheel, in order to build momentum and accelerate your business, you must do a series of consistent activities, exerting energy and effort until the flywheel begins to turn and gain momentum.

Think of your business as that flywheel circle with points of energy or momentum at the twelve o'clock, three o'clock, six o'clock, and nine o'clock marks. Each of those points represents an attribute of your business that is instrumental in propelling its success. Each represents a consistent action your organization must take to get your flywheel turning fast enough to drive tremendous acceleration.

As an example, let's look at DLP Real Estate Capital's flywheel. When we set out to determine our flywheel, it felt like a very difficult task, especially given the fact that we were running six or seven different businesses at the time. My executive team and I knew that there must be a few keys to our flywheel that, with the right amount of focus, would propel our growth. We spent a few hours in a conference room with a whiteboard mapping out our flywheel, and here is what we came up with:

DLP REAL ESTATE CAPITAL'S FLYWHEEL

At the twelve o'clock position, we have our first key action: *we offer great investment vehicles.*

At three o'clock, we set our second key action as: *we invest capital in providing housing solutions, leveraging the Elite Execution System.*

At the six o'clock position, we have: *we generate consistent superior returns with no losses.*

And finally, at nine o'clock, we have: *we grow our assets under management.*

This final key action, *growing our assets under management*, brings us back to the twelve o'clock position where *we offer great investment vehicles.*

Now, when we start spinning this wheel, those components all start to feed into one another as they increasingly build momentum, so much so that when you look at the story on the wheel, it's easy to see how each key action generates more and more momentum, more and more capital. This feeds into our ability to invest capital so we grow more investments under management. By taking those investments and managing them with no losses while generating superior returns—thanks to the Elite Execution System—you can see how we are able to raise more capital and, in turn, continue to offer great investment offerings.

Now think about the composition of your flywheel. What are the key components of your business that, when working in concert, deliver great value and propel it to build the momentum you need to grow?

THE ELITE ACCELERATION PLAN

Creating your flywheel is crucial to knowing what components create momentum and growth in your organization, but you still need to turn those concepts into strategies and systems that rapidly accelerate your revenue and sales. You can do this through implementation of the strategies set forth in the Elite Acceleration Plan, a tool that lays out a clear strategy and execution plan to achieve your growth targets. The plan—available with accompanying templates at DLPElite.com—can be broadly divided into two parts:

→ Strategy, which includes understanding whom you are selling to and what you are selling; defining your uncommon offering (how you differentiate your company and product); and determining your acceleration goals (where you want to go and what you want to achieve)

→ Execution, which involves eight core components to executing the Elite Acceleration Plan (we'll dive more into these components in the relevant section below)

ELITE ACCELERATION STRATEGY

Before you can focus on the nuts and bolts of your acceleration plan, it's important to develop a framework that clarifies who you are, whom you are selling to, what's unique about your product, and what you want the Elite Acceleration Plan to achieve (i.e., your revenue targets and key numbers). These are the conceptual components that your plan will be based on, so it's important to be crystal clear about them.

UNDERSTAND WHOM YOU ARE SELLING TO WHAT YOU ARE SELLING

When thinking of your acceleration plan, you need to be very clear on whom you are selling to. In other words, you need to define your core target audience.

Some people use the term *dream client* or *ideal customer*. I prefer the term *core client*. This is the person we want to provide value to. This is the person who will provide you with the most profitable path to growth.

If you are a company that has multiple business lines like DLP, you are going to have several different types of clients, and not all will be appropriate for every business offering. For example, the person who engages the services of our real estate brokerage to buy their first home is probably not going to be the accredited investors we target for our investment funds. Our core client would be someone we could target at a high level for all our businesses, someone who can help us scale.

At DLP, we have defined our core client as a principal owner with $5 million or more in assets and who has an interest in investing in investment housing. This is the type of accredited high net worth investor we target to invest capital into our funds, but it also defines the type of real estate investor we want to lend capital to via our lending business. This high net worth person with an interest in real estate—whether an active landlord, a homebuilder, or an investor—is also the person we want to provide brokerage services to.

When you are determining who your core client is, go as deeply as possible into their persona. Think about their defining characteristics—for example, age, profession, gender, life stage—and have this person in mind as you create your marketing messaging, your educational content, and your positioning and branding. This is your target. Know this person well.

Next, be clear on what it is you are actually selling. Although you may be selling an object, or you may be selling a service, first and foremost *you are selling a brand*. To be precise, *you are selling that brand's promise*.

Brand promises are the characteristics that your clients and potential clients associate with your product. You don't go out and market "these are our brand promises." Instead, these are the expectations, consciously or subconsciously, that people have when they do business with you. As I've mentioned, DLP's brand promises are that we guarantee results (execution), we provide speed (efficiency), and we deliver wow (great customer experience).

DEFINE YOUR UNCOMMON OFFERING

As you determine what your brand promises are, you want to be clear what your uncommon offering is. This starts with defining and owning your inside advantage, a concept coined by Robert Bloom in his book *Inside Advantage*.

Basically, Bloom says, your inside advantage *is* your uncommon offering. More widely used marketing terms for this are *the unique selling proposition* or *your unique product offering*.

Here is how I like to think of the inside advantage.

I imagine that all my competitors are standing next to each other on one large table, vying for the attention of the same client, all shouting in unison, "I offer a good product!"

Suddenly, one shouts out, "I offer the same product as everyone else but for five cents less!" In response, another says, "I will give you an extra 10 percent more of the same product for the same price!"

This continues for a while. All these competitors, standing side-by-side on the same big table, all of them essentially offering the same product, which they are all marketing in substantially the same way by simply offering better pricing or more product at a comparable price. Some might even create some slight variation to give the appearance of a difference, such as including free shipping or faster results.

So where am I?

I'm the guy on the other side of the room standing on my own little table saying, *I offer a different product.*

During the depths of the real estate recession, DLP Real Estate came up with an uncommon offering: the Elite Preferred Home Buyer Program. Everybody was nervous about the economy—home buyers were especially nervous about home values going down, about the economy, about their job security—and buyer's agents were in hot competition for the relatively little business that was out there.

With our Elite Preferred Home Buyer Program, if you bought a home with DLP Real Estate, we provided you with a whole range of benefits that nobody else offered. We paid for home inspections and termite inspections on each of our buyer client's homes so they would know what they were buying. We provided our buyers with a home warranty, and we guaranteed the lowest interest rate on their mortgages. We also provided the lowest cost on insurance, also guaranteed. But our biggest unique or uncommon value proposition was that we offered our clients a two-year "Love It or Leave It" guarantee. If they bought a home with us and, in the first two years, wanted to sell it for any reason—maybe they found a home they liked more elsewhere or lost their job and could no longer afford the home, or simply didn't like the home after all—we promised to buy that home back from them or sell it for free, their choice.

We took the majority of the stress out of the home-buying equation through this unique offering.

Once you know what your brand promise is and who your core client is, and you have created or defined your uncommon offering, it's time to move on to determining your acceleration goals.

DETERMINE YOUR ACCELERATION GOALS

Start by taking a look at the revenue targets in your Elite Compass: your Three-Year Aim and your One-Year Bull's-Eye. If you, for example, have a one-year revenue bull's-eye of $24 million and $6 million in net operating income, that will be where you start to calculate your acceleration goal for the year.

Next, determine the key numbers that you need to achieve in order to hit your revenue and net profitability numbers. Then work backward by determining how many units of product you need to sell to collect that $24 million in gross revenue. This is where you will need to delve into relevant data points.

For example, in my lending business, I look at what the loan volume has to be to generate the revenue I want to achieve, which is $24 million. I first look at as much past data as I can to determine our average revenue per loan so that I can identify the baseline number of loans we need to close to achieve our revenue goal. Then I look at what percentage of loan submissions close to determine how many loans we need to have submitted, then I determine the percentage of applications that turn into full loan submissions to determine how many applications we need. Then finally, I determine the number of leads or opportunities we need to achieve to get that number of loan applications. The formula would end up as: I need x leads to generate y applications to generate z loan submissions, which will provide x number of loans closed and loans volume to produce the $24 million in loans and the $6 million net operating income (NOI).

If you have the data, you can drill down even further to figure out how much traffic you need to drive to your website to produce the number of leads you need for the required number of applications. You can look at how many page views you need and how many followers on a particular social media platform.

Be careful, though. It's easy to get mired in so much data that you become overwhelmed or lose sight of why you are scrutinizing the data in the first place. There is so much information—such as how many likes you get on Facebook—that really provides no value other than, perhaps, validating that you are trending in the right direction. The possible data points are never ending, and not all lead to information that is useful or indicative of anything relevant to generating revenue.

Now that you know, based on a review and analysis of relevant data, how many leads you need to generate to reach your ultimate revenue goal—in my example, the $24 million in gross revenue—you have a framework for implementing an acceleration plan.

One last note about figuring out your past conversion rates: as you go through the information in this chapter, you may determine that you are going to shift and change your conversion rates as part of executing your Elite Acceleration Plan. You may decide that you are going to focus on higher quality leads, increase conversion from leads to application through sales training, increase the quality of your sales reps, or perhaps invest in better lead nurturing. If that's the case, you will want to use past data as a place to start and let it guide your plan forward in order to drive your revenue and profit targets.

ELITE ACCELERATION EXECUTION

At this point—thanks to your Elite Acceleration strategy—you understand what you are really selling and to whom, have isolated your uncommon offering, and have determined your acceleration goals. Now it is time to drive acceleration to achieve those goals through execution.

Execution on your acceleration strategy has eight core components:

→ Lead generation
→ Expert positioning and brand awareness
→ Business development
→ Sales enablement and resources
→ Sales hiring
→ Sales training

→ Sales management

→ Performance metrics and data

LEAD GENERATION

The goal of lead generation is to provide the sales team with a consistent flow of leads to turn into clients and, in turn, to enable your organization to achieve its revenue goals.

Leads, based on how they are generated, fall into four types: paid, owned, earned, and shared.

→ Paid leads—ones you attract by buying the opportunity to reach your target audiences—can be generated through:
  » Digital advertising, including paid searches (paying to be at the top of Google search results, for example); social media advertising on platforms such as Facebook, LinkedIn, or Instagram; and display or retargeting ads (including banner ads on a website or a blog, for example);
  » Traditional advertising, including direct mail, print media ads in newspapers, magazines, and so forth; and broadcast (television and radio); or
  » Sponsorships of for-profit or nonprofit organizations and events
→ Owned leads are the ones that come to you directly via the platforms you own. They might be gathered through your website, your collateral materials, email marketing campaigns, and the original content you produce by publishing blogs, white papers, webinars, and podcasts, to name a few.
→ Earned leads are relationship based. They could come from organic (nonpaid) internet searches as a result of SEO

(search engine optimization) efforts; from media coverage, from influencer promotions, or other sources stemming from public relations or other publicity-based outreach efforts. You put your name and product information out there, a vehicle for distributing your information picks it up, and someone sees or reads the information you circulated and contacts you.

→ Shared leads are those you receive through social media platform such as Facebook, LinkedIn, Twitter, Instagram, and YouTube. Shared leads come from you creating some form of content that is interesting enough for strangers to share it—this includes videos, posts, tweets, or any other form of content—to their followers who then, in turn, either contact you and become a lead or even share it with their followers who become leads.

Developing Your Lead-Generation Plan

Developing your lead-generation plan is an iterative process. Figuring out the plan that gets you to your revenue and profit targets while producing the volume and quality of leads you need to propel your acceleration formula is challenging and doesn't happen in a vacuum. As you work to figure out how to best generate leads for your particular business as cost effectively as possible, you will simultaneously need to focus on the other components of the acceleration plan—expert positioning and lead conversion, which largely comes from improving sales management and training, and so on—in order to achieve your goals. The basics of a lead-generation plan are:

1. Determine your targeted lead quantity. How many leads do you need to achieve your revenue goals?

2. Determine your targeted per lead cost. How much does the average lead cost?

3. Determine your budget allocation. The number of leads multiplied by the per lead cost will provide you with a budget, or at least the baseline of a budget.

4. Determine your lead source strategy. This is the meat of lead generation, how and where are you going to generate the leads you need to achieve your revenue goals. This is where you dig deep into the four types of leads discussed earlier and determine how and where you are going to generate these leads that fit your overall budget.

In order to execute on a lead-generation plan, you must produce and distribute content. That is where Expert Positioning and Brand Awareness comes in on your journey of building your acceleration plan.

EXPERT POSITIONING AND BRAND AWARENESS

Today is the information age. Over the last two years alone, 90 percent of the data in the world has been generated. Think about that. This is exciting and incredible. It also means it has never been harder to differentiate yourself and get the attention of your prospective clients. There are so many people and companies fighting for their attention; it has never been harder to stand out and get your company noticed.

Creating and distributing content that gets the attention of your target clients is by far the hottest topic in marketing. There is so much information out there and so many experts with a different spin on content marketing that it can be overwhelming. What is even more overwhelming is the endless options of social channels and platforms to attempt to distribute your content and get noticed by your target clients.

I am going to attempt to simplify all the noise around content or inbound marketing into what I believe to be the critical decisions and actions you need to take in order to gain and keep the attention of your prospective and existing core clients.

The first big step is to determine what you are the expert at, or potentially what you are going to become the expert on. People want to receive their information from experts. With all of the noise—the high number of blogs, videos, social posts, books, and articles on virtually every topic—it is more important than ever that you position yourself as THE EXPERT in your business or in the challenge that your core client is facing and that your company will be able to help solve. You need to become the authority on the topic. In order to position yourself as the expert, you need to create and distribute content to your core clients that makes your expertise clear.

Creating the Right Content

Before you decide what form of content you are going to create and how you plan to distribute it, you must first decide why you are creating the content in the first place. What purpose do you want your content to have? In essence, all content is storytelling. You want to convey the story of your company, your product or solution, your clients, or your industry with the purpose of positioning yourself as an expert so that people want to do business with you. This is how you leverage content to generate leads and opportunities.

When you set out to create content, you want to think about

all content as part of a content campaign. The fundamentals of a content campaign are:

1. Setting the goal of the campaign
2. Determining the brand awareness of your target audience
3. Choosing a content theme and pillar keywords
4. Creating the cluster of content that will support your content theme

Goal of the Campaign

The overarching goal of any content campaign should be to generate leads and/or close sales. The specific goals of a campaign may vary, though, based on your current acceleration goals. Are you focusing on generating new leads or incubating existing leads? Are you focusing on generating first-time clients or repeat clients? Are you focusing on one specific product or all of your products? Are you trying to build the top of funnel—essentially, obtain new leads—or are you expecting to actually close sales through the campaign?

Based on the goals of the campaign, you need to choose a call to action that will drive those goals.

Creating Your Call to Action

Not every single *piece* of content needs to have a strong call to action, but you do need a powerful call to action in every campaign. Call to actions can take many forms. If you're looking to obtain a reader's contact information, then it may take the form of a free report or registering for a web-based or live event. It could also be to schedule a one-on-one meeting, or you may be simply presenting an offer to buy your product as the call to action.

Regardless of what you are asking your content consumer to do, you need to make sure that your call to action—or the ask—matches the customer's need and stage in the discovery and decision process. Pushing someone who lands on your website for the first time to buy your product or to schedule a meeting may not be a practical next step for that prospect. Instead, the incremental action of joining a webinar or downloading a report may be the right next step.

Finally, when it comes to content, do not be afraid to sell in your marketing. Converting leads into sales is the goal of your content marketing after all. Just make sure that the ratio of the value you are providing to any requests to purchase stay around three to one, meaning you provide value in your content for free at least three times as often as you are soliciting a sale.

Brand Awareness

When you are creating and distributing a content campaign, it is critical that the content and the call to action matches the stage of the buyer and their awareness with your brand or company. If you are producing and distributing content that is primarily going to be consumed by new visitors—potential clients who do not know your company—you will want different content than if you are generating material for existing clients or for active prospects who have been aware of your company and engaged with your marketing and sales team.

As a content marketer, you are looking to move people through the process of starting as a visitor—those who come across your company for the first time—to becoming a prospect who is now aware of your company, to becoming an active prospect who is engaged in your content, learning about your company and possibly also in communication with the sales team, to becoming a customer, and then ultimately to becoming an advocate who is promoting your company online and offline.

In order to generate visitors, you are going to create awareness content—examples are blogs, articles, and ads—that will get someone to click to learn more. Then the next step is educational content, such as whitepapers, webinars, forums, and email marketing. These are often calls to action to obtain contact information. Then the next stage after education is selection. This content is designed to help the prospect choose or select your company. This includes sales-enablement content such as sales presentations, product analysis or comparison, and case studies.

The final type of content is training content, such as workshops, videos, tutorials, FAQs, and other support content. This is designed primarily for your customer or clients.

Content Pillar

A content pillar is a substantive and usually informative piece of content on a specific topic or theme that can be broken into many smaller pieces or forms of content. Examples of content pillars include e-books, reports, and guides. These content pillars are often the call to actions of the content campaign and should be focused on solving a problem or providing critical information around a top priority of your target audience.

By focusing your attention and energy on creating a single

content pillar, it's easy to break that finished piece into blog posts, infographics, videos, emails, social media posts, and ads to attract potential clients through different channels.

Developing a content pillar first makes it much easier to develop a campaign that is going to achieve the desired results. It will simplify your content creation and distribution efforts, as well as increase your conversion results when done well. In addition, it makes it easier for you—or whoever the business leader is who is involved in the content creation—to concentrate on developing one great piece of content, and then not be as involved in producing the rest of the content pieces.

Even as we have grown the DLP family of businesses, I remain involved in the content as I am still the face of the company and I am an expert on our products and our clients. I have found that by putting my focus on developing the content theme and pillar content, I can have a lot of influence and add a lot of value to our content strategy without then needing to be involved in every single content piece, which could hold up content production or distribution. This has saved me a lot of time and tremendously helped our marketing team.

Content Cluster

After you finalize your pillar content, the next step is to produce all the content pieces that will complement this pillar. This is called content clusters, also known as topic clusters. Through content clusters, you build groups of related content, such as blog posts, emails, videos, and infographics around a specific topic, your pillar content. Think of the cluster content as subtopics. This is a powerful strategy to position yourself as an expert, drive visitors and prospects to your content pillar and call to action, all while helping drive SEO. Content clustering is an excellent way to build free organic search traffic, especially if you utilize keywords effectively throughout your campaign. It is important that in your content clustering you are using linking to drive traffic to the other content in the cluster, especially the pillar content.

Distributing Content

Creating content, however, is only the first part of your marketing campaign. The second part entails determining how you are going to distribute your content. The act of creating content is of very little value if the content does not get into the hands of potential clients, the people who need the content and, ultimately, who will need and/or want your product. This is where the four sources of leads come into play—paid, earned, shared, and owned—that we discussed earlier.

You may choose to pay to distribute your content by running a pay-per-click (PPC) campaign via a search engine or reaching out to potential content consumers through social media advertising (using Facebook or Instagram, for example), or by running banner ads on third-party websites, or even through traditional print, radio, or television advertising.

You might opt for distributing your content through your owned resources, such as your email list, website, blog, social media pages, and channels to drive traffic to your website while also bolstering your site's internet ranking (through the use of SEO), making it easier to find through a Google search.

Maybe you will opt to promote your content or product by going on a third-party podcast, emailing the database of an influencer, or producing content that is so remarkable that others will organically share it with their own social networks.

Keep in mind that the goal of creating and distributing content is to generate more business. No matter how good your content or information is, if you do not make it easy for people to understand what you can offer them and how to contact you, all of your effort will be pointless. The point of content marketing is to drive people to take action, including at a minimum to provide you with their contact information, so that you can continue to provide value and, in turn, create more opportunities to present your product.

THE TRUTH ABOUT LEAD CONVERSION

When we discuss acceleration and growing revenue, as we have been throughout this chapter, most business leaders believe their biggest priority is generating more leads or at bats. The reality, however, is most high-growth companies have a greater opportunity right in front of them: converting the leads and opportunities they already have.

Salespeople often claim that their biggest problem is the quantity of leads they are receiving. This is not usually the case. In my experience, salespeople very often follow up with a lead only one or two times, despite the fact that most sales conversions happen after the eighth contact.

Ideally, your team members are calling leads within five minutes of the lead being received or, worst-case scenario, within the hour. In fact, studies show that lead conversion increases by more than 1,000 percent when the lead is called within the first fifteen minutes of contact. This is Lead Conversion 101.

In a lead generation and management platform I owned a number of years ago, I had access to the CRM data of more than one hundred successful sales teams with more than two thousand sales reps who, combined, had literally millions of leads. Nearly 50 percent of those leads had not been called in over a year. When new leads came in, the average time it took for the sales rep to reach out with a first phone call was right about twenty-four hours. In other words, the sales teams were not working their leads or opportunities effectively.

Many organizations still regard lead conversion as the sole job of sales. It's that old-fashioned line of demarcation where marketing generates leads and sales converts them. This is far from the reality of what it takes to win business today. The marketing team needs to continue to assist with keeping relevant content flowing to leads. The marketing team can assist the sales team through additional sales enablement tools, such as auto dialers, alerts and tracking when prospects read your content or emails, prebuilt email and text templates to make lead response faster, nurture campaigns based on the stage of the prospect, and a well-built CRM that supports the sales reps and makes their jobs easier.

BUSINESS DEVELOPMENT

Most organizations lump business development in with sales, treating the two areas of acceleration as if they were one and the same. The reality is that business development is as much (if not more) about marketing or lead generation as it is about sales. In fact, the *Oxford English Dictionary* (see Lexico.com) defines business development as "the activity of pursuing strategic opportunities for a particular business or organization, for example by cultivating partnerships or other commercial relationships, or identifying new markets for its products or services."

CREATING A BUSINESS DEVELOPMENT TEAM

The ability to develop business is arguably the most critical and valuable skill benefiting any high-growth organization. Being able to find new strategic relationships or core clients and then being able to create the necessary awareness and urgency to close those relationships is an amazing skillset. If you are fortunate to be both proficient in and passionate about business development, you may want to retain this core responsibility yourself, at least during your early growth period.

At some point in your path of scaling your business, however, you will probably need to invest in building at least a small business development team, even though hiring, managing, and retaining talented business development team members can be very challenging, not to mention very expensive. Building an elite business development team is a lot of work, but if you hire great people and stay committed, you will realize multiple returns.

Events and Trade Shows

A common component of business development strategies is attending industry events and trade shows. I have found attending events to be a great way to conduct multiple face-to-face meetings in just a day or two that would otherwise take a lot of time and traveling. Industry events are a great way to build your brand; consider offering your services as a speaker, participating in panels, and having your company maintain a booth. In addition, these events present valuable opportunities to meet and recruit talent.

Depending on your business, hosting your own events can also be an extremely effective business development tool. At DLP Capital Partners, we hold events quarterly for high net worth investors in each of the three markets we are in, in addition to holding two large retreat-type events each year.

Business development, in essence, is simply about getting in front of prospective core clients. This generally is not as difficult as you may think. It really just requires taking consistent action. You have to identify where or how to recognize potential core clients, such as going to industry events or finding targeted lists. You can find targeted lists in a number of ways, from acquiring the data from a data provider, to figuring out who your competitor's clients are, finding online lists such as lists of companies that won awards, and looking at the attendance list of industry events. Once you find prospective core clients, it is just a matter of getting their attention. This can be done through simply picking up the phone, writing a handwritten card, sending an email, posting on social media, or using press releases. A great book on the concept of contact marketing is *How to Get a Meeting with Anyone* by Stu Heinecke. The book will simplify and demystify business development.

SALES ENABLEMENT

The next acceleration area is sales enablement, which involves determining what resources the sales team needs so they can go out and sell. Do they need a presentation deck? Brochures and fliers? Website landing pages and email nurture campaigns? This is where sales and marketing need to be on the same page. It may be marketing's job to produce the resources for the sales team, but they are going to need guidance from the sales team so they can deliver what the sales team needs in order to convert leads into sales.

SALES HIRING

Creating a great sales team entails a lot more than just hiring people and training them on your selling system. How are you going to attract the right salespeople? What is your plan to provide appropriate training, management, and resources so you are setting your salespeople up to succeed in converting those leads, bringing in new clients, and driving revenue and profitability? This fifth area in executing your Elite Acceleration Plan—sales hiring—is vital to your company's growth.

Sales hiring starts first with determining what type of sales organization you want to build. Are you going to build a centralized inside-sales organization, with the leads being generated for your sales reps? Or are you going to build a team of hunters who generate their own leads? Next, consider what type of sales professional is best for your organization. The following are examples of questions that may help you determine what type of sales reps you want to hire:

→ Would hiring experienced industry veterans be the best

strategy, or would you prefer to hire less experienced reps from your industry?

→ Should you consider seeking out proven sales professionals from other industries, with the idea of capitalizing on their proven track records in other types of businesses?

→ Would you rather hire reps without experience who have a clean slate and do not have bad habits?

→ Are you hiring reps to work inbound leads via an inside-sales approach, or do you want outside reps who are going to be doing a lot of face-to-face appointments?

→ Do you need reps who are particularly skilled at converting cold leads, or are you feeding reps only warm leads?

→ Where do you want your team located? Do you want to centralize your salesforce, or do you prefer a geographically scattered team?

→ Do you want reps who are looking for a long-term career?

→ Are you going to pay them as W-2 team members with a salary and benefits, or are you looking for reps who will work on a 1099 straight commission basis?

Once you have a good understanding of the type of reps you want to hire, where you plan to locate them, and how you plan to pay them, you can follow the hiring process covered in chapter 3 to attract sales professionals who match what you are looking for.

SALES TRAINING

Training your sales team is critical in driving your acceleration plan. Building a world-class sales team requires a lot of time and effort.

Creating Your Training Program

You will need to provide your sales associates with detailed training on your company, your products, how your pricing works, your CRM and any other technology tools your sales team uses on customer service, as well as on your sales process. This could include training on prospecting, scripting, how to deliver your sales presentation, how and when to follow up on leads and, with existing customers, how to overcome objections, and how to ask for and close the sale. If you are highly skilled in sales, all this may come easy to you; however, if you are not proficient in sales yourself, I recommend that you leverage your top salespeople to help you.

Another great way for you to build your training program is to leverage some of the great sales experts and their books. Some of my favorites include:

→ *The Only Sales Guide You'll Ever Need* by Anthony Iannarino
→ *New Sales. Simplified* by Mike Weinberg
→ *The Conversion Code* by Chris Smith
→ *Fanatical Prospecting* by Jeb Blount
→ *The Ultimate Sales Machine* by Chet Holmes
→ *The 10X Rule* by Grant Cardone

Be sure to take the time to document and record your trainings, build tools, and incorporate quizzes or tests. Utilizing a system like thinkific.com to be your training platform, not just for sales but also for your entire organization, can be an incredible investment in the growth and success of your organization.

I also highly recommend that you engage your sales team in regular role-playing, which is a great way to actually test your team members' skills and understanding of the trainings. If you skip the step of role-playing, you will often find that reps do not have the confidence to put the trainings into action. Role-playing can be uncomfortable, but it will help your team build the confidence and comfort to put the skills they were trained on into action.

How Much Training Is Enough?

It is important to consider how much to train and how often.

If you hire less experienced sales reps, you are going to need to provide more training. I recommend creating an intense sales onboarding program for all new reps that lasts anywhere from two to four weeks. Putting in this sort of time and effort to train your reps in the beginning can make a significant impact on the short-term and long-term probability of success of a new sales rep.

Keep in mind that training is something that needs to be ongoing. I recommend having a minimum of one training per week for all sales reps and providing additional training for reps who are struggling in any specific area.

I also recommend taking your favorite sales books and using them to train your sales staff. My sales team and I have together, over a period of a couple of months, read several of the sales books mentioned previously, training on one or two chapters each week. I have found this to be an extremely effective way to train sales reps.

SALES MANAGEMENT

Another critical aspect of growing a successful sales team so you can accelerate your business growth is sales management, the seventh component in executing your Elite Acceleration Plan.

Sales management is difficult. It takes a lot of time and effort. What's more, great sales managers are hard to find or develop. Great sales managers know that the difference between highly successful salespeople and the rest of the sales force is activity, massive amounts of action and time spent prospecting to get in front of potential customers and then, once you have their attention, time spent actually interacting with them.

Even though the importance of spending time on prospecting and developing customer relationships might seem obvious, the fact is that most sales teams are filled with salespeople who do not spend the majority of their time doing these activities. They find tons of distractions and excuses to do just about anything and everything other than prospecting for and being in front of their prospects.

When they do prospect and go on sales appointments, these sales reps often skip steps, do not ask for the sale, and then do not follow up. They do not log notes and follow-up activities in the CRM right away, and later they get busy and forget.

There is only one real solution to these issues, and that is good sales management, which hinges on building relationships with the sales reps while setting clear goals and providing them with the tools they need to achieve those goals.

A good sales manager knows that accountability is at the

center of all management. Reps need to know they will be held accountable not just for results but also for the lead measures that drive results. This includes meeting the requirements for number of phone calls made, number of "spoke withs" reported, number of applications filled out, and number of appointments set.

A good manager consistently builds alignment and ensures accountability through consistent coaching and one-on-one meetings. This should include "windshield" time—time spent actually out in the field with the rep observing their performance and then following up with coaching and training. With inside sales reps, this means being on the phone with them, listening in, and then follow-up coaching.

Sales management includes hiring, training, and sometimes firing sales reps. When managing a sales team, you have to consider the effects each team member has on the overall salesforce. Keeping underperformers around can hurt your performers in that it may demotivate them. In addition, if you keep your underperformers on, you are providing them with leads and opportunities that could go to your performers or to new reps who will become performers. Keeping around sales reps who bring drama and negativity, are always complaining, who do not show up to training, or do not use the company's approach or tools can have a major negative effect on the entire sales team.

Finding the Right Sales Manager

If you are the owner of your business, then you either need to commit to being the sales manager, find someone within your organization to take on the sales management role, or recruit a sales manager from outside.

Be cautious about turning one of your top sales reps into your sales manager. It is nearly impossible to have a top salesperson keep up their sales numbers while managing a team. If you take your top sales rep out of sales to manage, you will lose one of your top sales producers. Furthermore, many of the skills and traits that made that top sales rep successful can actually work against them in sales management. The skills necessary to succeed in sales management—such as the ability to focus on others, the ability to create heroes rather than being the hero, and the ability to coach and train others—are often not the strengths of a top sales rep. I recommend utilizing a personality profile such as The Predictive Index—something we covered in chapter 3—to evaluate your top sales rep against the requirements and expectations you would have for a sales manager.

PERFORMANCE METRICS AND DATA

The final component of executing your Elite Acceleration Plan concerns measuring your marketing and sales teams' efforts with performance metrics and data.

Once you have a plan in place to generate sufficient lead volume and you know how you are going to attract, train, and manage the right sales team, you need a way to measure the results of your acceleration efforts with very clear, quantifiable, and actionable performance metrics. This is the only way to ensure that your marketing and sales teams are performing to the standards your organization requires for meaningful acceleration.

You will need to examine each of the key metrics across the sales process from beginning to end so you can track and analyze the data across the various stages of a sale—from the moment a prospect first becomes aware of your organization to the time it takes them to become a client to the point where they become an advocate.

In order to manage your sales and marketing systems, you will need to make sure you are setting up the mechanisms to track data—such as making sure your website is set up appropriately to report Google Analytics—and then make sure that the data is retrievable on demand and also tied into your CRM.

You need to be able to follow a data trail all the way from marketing spend to closed deal and all the touch points in between so that you can determine what is working and what needs realignment. If you don't have the in-house expertise to support this function, go with a reputable outside vendor. The only way to keep an acceleration program moving forward is by constantly assessing performance based on sound metrics. You need to know what works, what doesn't, which salespeople are productive, and who is not meeting expectations.

SUMMARY

Accelerating the growth of your business requires a disciplined, consistent, action-oriented plan. I encourage you to design and execute your Elite Acceleration Plan piece by piece.

Keep a clear focus on whom you want to sell your products to and how you are going to deliver your uncommon offering. By promoting your product or offering through whatever marketing channels are the likeliest to generate leads, you will set a strong foundation for acceleration. And remember that most companies have plenty of leads or opportunities. The one thing that sets scalable companies apart from the competition is that they spend all the time necessary to nurture the leads and opportunities and convert them to closed sales.

Of course, the key to growth does not stop here. Keeping existing clients is the best and most cost-effective way to generate new business. In the next chapter, we will cover the Elite Execution System approach to customer experience.

CHAPTER TWELVE

DELIVERING WOW

Every company claims to focus on customer experience (CX), but the reality is that very few organizations give any real thought to whether or how they are providing great CX.

When people think of CX, they think about how the customer gets treated at the point of the sale or the fulfillment of the product or service. Everyone wants to deliver great service and to give a great experience when they're selling something to someone. And the focus on CX usually ends there.

This type of attitude toward customer service and CX is outdated, especially if you are trying to grow your business.

The reality is that the CX is a part of every way, shape, and form that anyone affiliated with your business comes in contact with a customer or potential customer.

What your office waiting room looks like is part of CX. How your staff answers the phone—and whether and for how long people are put on hold—is part of CX. CX is certainly part of the sales and delivery process, but it is also the impression the company makes through its website and what kind of reviews it has on multiple online platforms. CX even emanates from your company's internal culture, because how you treat your own people informs the world's perception of your brand.

CX and team member experience (EX) are so closely related that it is hard to find a clear line of demarcation. The lines between brand and culture are all but erased, which is why internal image needs to match external image. This is something that can only happen when companies actually are who and what they say they are.

One of DLP's core values is "Enthusiastically delivering wow." CX—the commitment to delivering that wow—is not just something we do; it is at the core of who we are as a company. We go above and beyond to delight and amaze everyone we encounter, and that includes potential customers, current customers, members of our community, and equally as important, our internal staff.

The more that our internal way of behaving and communicating matches our external way of marketing and selling, the more this informs how we deliver services to our customers. And that results in the ability to provide a great CX, translating into growth and profit.

In today's economy, with the amount of competition most businesses face, providing great CX is one of the areas where you can seriously differentiate your company and bring tremendous value to your organization, to your customers, and to the growth of your brand. The flip side of that is also true. If you fail to focus on CX, you will feel the financial fallout. This is why, if you haven't given any serious thought to how to promote your company and your brand by leveraging customer service, it is time to shift your internal paradigm and start purposefully positioning your company to deliver a great experience to everyone it comes in contact with.

THE FRONTLINE OBSESSION

In order to consistently deliver that wow kind of CX at DLP, we knew we had to develop what we call our frontline obsession. In other words, we needed our senior leaders to be obsessed with what happens at each point of communication with the customer, wherever and whenever that interaction occurred.

What happens at the front line is absolutely critical to your organization's success. Too often, owners and senior leaders lose touch with the nitty-gritty on-the-ground details of how the business is run. They are so far removed up the ladder from the origin of customer complaints that by the time they get wind of an issue, it's gone through so many layers of messaging and interpretation that all perspectives on the problem have been skewed.

We stress the importance of our senior leaders staying in touch with the front line. We expect senior management to visit the properties, pick up the phone and answer customer calls, and check out any negative online reviews or feedback. There should never be multiple degrees of separation between the information our frontline folks receive and what our senior managers can relate to firsthand.

Having a frontline obsession means getting everyone in the trenches working alongside each other. It means all the support coordinators, receptionists, technicians, construction workers, salespeople, as well as executives are equally involved in identifying and addressing company problems.

Sticking to chains of command—where, for example, a senior leader talks to a manager who talks to the coordinator and then filters that information back up and brings it to meetings—creates, in my experience, inefficiency and costly delays. It fosters an extremely skewed and inaccurate perception of reality, or at least of the customer's reality.

Customer service should never be considered a lower rung responsibility. It is everyone's responsibility. A number of years back, we created a chief experience officer position at DLP. This person's sole focus is making sure that the experience internally throughout the organization, and externally, is everything that we hope it to be, that we're truly delighting, amazing, and delivering wow to our customers and our team members each and every day.

Placing this level of emphasis on the CX isn't just something that helps us look a little better or do a better job at reacting to complaints. If you're delivering wow to your customers and you're delivering wow to your team members, you're going to be turning clients or customers into advocates. Advocates come back to you again and again. And that, it turns out, increases profits in a verifiable and measurable way.

In chapter 7, when discussing Rocks, I relayed a story about a recurring problem DLP was having with expediting apartment turnover. DLP has more than twenty-five thousand residents living in our apartment communities, and somewhere close to one thousand people move into one of our apartments each and every month. It's a large job getting all those apartments into move-in-ready condition.

There is urgency to turn the apartments over quickly because every day the apartment is not occupied translates into lost revenue to the company. We have a large number of team members, contractors, and other partners whose schedules depend on our being quick and organized in our management of these turnovers.

We started trying to address this problem early on in our property management business. Several senior leaders were involved, and we had meeting after meeting as everyone worked to find a way to improve on the turnover process. We had the president of the property management division meeting with the head of operations, the regional service supervisor, the director of operations, the regional property manager, and the CFO, to name just a few.

We would end up rushing the apartment prep, which resulted in new residents being dissatisfied with the state of their new apartments, resulting in a chain reaction of customer complaints, maintenance and other service calls, more than a few unflattering reviews on social media, and untold amounts of lost potential customers from diminished goodwill.

Before this got out of hand, I organized a big all-hands meeting to deal with these issues. Against pushback from my senior staff, who insisted that they could handle the problem and that frontline folks were needed in the field, I brought in all the service technicians and the leasing agents involved in this part of the business.

These frontline staff brought the real-life feedback that we needed to hear. They were able to explain what was actually happening, what the real challenges were, and were able to suggest some very small and simple ways that we could improve the process. They had been trying to tell us how to fix the problem the whole time, but nobody was listening.

We incorporated their suggestions into our process, and in a very short time, our turnover time was cut down dramatically, as were the number of complaints. But as importantly, listening to the front line and including them in decisions empowered them and made them happier. This translated into them giving even better service to our customers. It helped them to feel more pride about their work.

I can easily equate hundreds of thousands of dollars in additional revenue and avoid lost time directly to this meeting and the actions taken from the meeting. The simple act of involving the frontline people and asking for and respecting their opinions made a dramatic difference to the experience and the service we're able to deliver to the customer.

CREATING CX ADVOCATES AND AMBASSADORS

Another great consequence of solving the rental turnover problem was that every team member involved in that process, every contractor whose time was respected, and every new resident whose apartment was perfect became a potential ambassador for our company.

This type of relationship building is priceless, especially in this day and age where most business feels transactional. When your customers and your clients feel so connected to your company that they act as your ambassadors, you know that you are on the right track and that you are driving significant short-term and long-term gain to the organization. This is when you are going to see your organization soar in terms of revenue and profitability. Often, this is where the turning point to significant growth and scale will start to happen.

We all know how expensive it is to acquire new clients. In many organizations, marketing costs from 20 percent to 40 percent of revenue. One of the most rewarding aspects of committing to exemplary CX is that, along with continuing to do business with you, your current customers will encourage others to do the same. They will provide referrals to friends, family members, and colleagues. When you can get people to be your ambassador and bring in business that you don't have to pay for, you are looking at incredible profit, not to mention a typically easier sales cycle. It's just about the best thing that can happen.

This is why it is so important to have an actual proactive plan to encourage referrals from customers and team members.

There's an old saying: No one cares how much you know until they know how much you care. What are you doing right now to make sure that your existing customers and clients know you care? I'm not talking about spending a whole lot of money, but are you doing anything to show your appreciation for their business? Are you sending them notes on their birthdays? Do you send them handwritten thank-you cards? Do you provide them gifts at closing, or at the transaction, or at any point after the sale? Are your clients shocked or amazed by how your organization consistently goes above and beyond? Are they taken aback by your thoughtfulness and attention to the smallest details?

There are many ways to keep in touch with your customers and show your appreciation, such as sending a special gift around the holidays, holding a client appreciation party, or supporting a community event or charity that is important to them. Just picking up the phone to check in with them and ask how you can help support them or enhance their experience, to let them know what is new and exciting with your company, can go a long way. These are all ways to deliver wow.

In the same vein, you need to also make sure your team members know you care about them, to make sure you're enriching their lives, making their lives easier, giving them reasons to smile. Team members are your best ambassadors because they see firsthand what kind of company you have and how much you care about your customers. Make them proud and they will make you proud by shouting your company's praises to the world.

Even people who don't do direct business or work with you can become advocates for your business. Every touch point with a potential customer or potential hire is an opportunity to sell your brand and recruit an ambassador. Some of the very best advocates I've had over the years have been potential team members whom I didn't hire but who were so appreciative of and impressed with their experience with us and our organization that they're still out there recommending us to others.

And don't forget friends and family members and their friends. It's amazing how many people we all know within one or two degrees of separation, how easily people can connect. Positioning your business and your brand as a place where great CX is a given, where people will always get the wow, really is the gift that keeps on giving.

ONLINE REVIEWS: GOOD, BAD, AND UGLY

I can't remember the last time I've gone to a restaurant without first checking the online reviews. I don't rent a movie, download a book, choose a hotel, or buy pretty much anything unless I've checked the reviews. I don't care what the company says, or what the critics say, or what the professionals claim; I want to know what the customers before me think. And I know that my clients and customers are exactly the same.

More than 70 percent of buying decisions are made before you ever speak to a potential client. By the time someone in your organization actually has a conversation that could lead to a business transaction, the person has likely been to your website and read your content, checked you out on Facebook, perused your LinkedIn profile, and done a thorough review of Google, Yelp, and any trade industry-relevant website reviews. By the time your sales staff gets the opportunity to say word one about your company, your potential customer has already formed an impression of who you are and what you do.

And if that impression is negative, you'll never know it because you won't have the opportunity to get that up close and personal in the first place. You're not getting a chance to deliver your wow because you've been thrown to the curb based on impressions brought forth through your online image.

You need to take control of your online image so the reviews don't completely control you. Your approaches need to be both proactive and reactive.

It's likely that your organization has received reviews on several different platforms, particularly Google, Facebook, and Yelp. Keep in mind that no matter how great the CX you provide, there will always be people who leave negative reviews. And, unfortunately, just a few negative reviews can skew your overall rating. Most people won't take the time to actually read a lot of reviews, so if they see, for example, that you have three out of five stars on Google, they are going to move on to a competitor. It can also be a black mark against your company if you have too few reviews. People are wary of a company that seems under the internet radar. This is why it is important that you take a very proactive approach to collecting as many positive reviews as possible.

Even if you are giving your clients amazing service, they are not going to leave great reviews unless you ask them to. Make it as easy as possible for them to let the world know how great you are.

There are a lot of great companies out there that can help you gather up reviews and make the process a little bit easier. We use a site right now called GatherUp.com that sends people a link to leave reviews. One of our companies, DLP Realty, has the link DLPreviews.com. Leaving feedback about our companies or services is as simple as clicking on that link.

As often as possible, we try to do this live with them while we're at the closing table or on the phone. We send the link by email as well.

We've done promotions over the years—such as giving away Starbucks gift cards—to encourage people to leave reviews, but typically we just ask for reviews whenever we can. We do this at our properties all the time. A service technician, leasing agent, or the property manager might ask a resident to leave a quick five-star review, and the resident will use their phone or we will offer to let them use our iPad or, if they're at the office, our computer. It's a matter of keeping it top of mind and making it a regular part of the communications cycle.

We encourage our team members to do this by running contests for who gets the most five-star reviews. We offer some pretty nice prizes, such as $100 gift cards or a weekend vacation. The response has been amazing.

We've built getting good reviews into our culture. We've seen rental communities that we've acquired go from two-star ratings when we buy the property up to four-and-a-half-star ratings, and it's amazing how we see occupancy soar from that alone. The amount of traffic and the amount of people submitting inquiries about renting our apartments has gone up dramatically for these properties because people are no longer losing interest by reading negative reviews.

Dealing with negative reviews can be a bigger challenge. Even if they have nothing to do with your abilities or the services you offer, negative reviews can damage your business.

Make sure you respond to every negative review even if it's completely bogus or inaccurate. You should do everything you can to show the rest of the world that you're actively responding, that you are engaged, and that you care.

Next, do what you can to get the review removed. For example, if someone leaves a scathing review because they paid a fifty-dollar fee to apply for one of our apartments but they were turned down because they didn't qualify, we will offer to refund their fee if they agree to take down the review. We do what we can even if it looks like we are bribing people, because the negative publicity costs us far more than the fifty-dollar refund. We also will ramp up our requests for more positive reviews to bury the negative one and raise our overall rating back up.

We also carefully monitor and actively seek reviews on Glassdoor, the site most visited by job seekers. I recommend making sure your existing team members are going on Glassdoor to talk about their great experiences at your company and provide positive reviews. If you do get negative reviews from a previous team member, be sure to respond and reach out to the person to get those reviews removed if possible.

Also, keep your LinkedIn page up to date, and make sure all your team members are linked to your corporate page and are out there being ambassadors for the organization on their pages.

Managing your internet reputation takes constant vigilance, but it's an important part of business today.

As long as you focus on delivering wow internally to your team and externally to your clients, amazing things will happen for the growth of your organization.

CONCLUSION

How do you eat an elephant?

One bite at a time.

The thought of implementing all the elements of the Elite Execution System at once is going to feel a lot like taking on a giant elephant-sized meal, but don't let that deter you. You don't have to consume every piece of the system at the same time.

What I have tried to provide in these pages is a blueprint, a clear path to travel as you work to scale your organization, so you can grow your revenue and increase your profits for many years to come.

Look to the four quadrants of the operating system—Strategy, Operations, People, and Acceleration—and work your way through them using the tools provided throughout this book.

Start with determining your core values, your purpose, your mission statement, and your BHAG. Get honest about where your business is today and how a lack of discipline might be keeping you from forging ahead.

Then use the Elite Compass to plan out the strategy for achieving your BHAG, your seven-year checkpoint, your Three-Year Aim, and your One-Year Bull's-Eye. Evaluate your business and set goals through the lenses of the four quadrants of your business—Strategy, People, Operations, and Acceleration.

Begin putting the disciplines in place to make sure you get there: achieving your Rocks and WIGs, solving your teams' issues through IDS, building leadership and engagement throughout your organization utilizing the Elite Alignment Workbook, and the alignment huddles and meetings to drive ownership and accountability while building trust and lasting relationships.

All you need to get started is disciplined thought and a commitment to developing an Elite Organization. Once you are reasonably clear on where you are going, you can build an organization filled with Rock Star A Players who share your core values and want to be a part of achieving your mission. As long as you march forward twenty miles a day, every day, you will succeed. As long as you back up your strategy with disciplined action and disciplined people, you will grow your business in ways you can only imagine. You will build a truly great organization that transcends you, that can and will weather any market cycle, and that will achieve sustained growth and profitability over many decades.

Keep spreading this disciplined approach to your sales and marketing and to the products and value you deliver to your customers and clients. Provide a wow experience to your customers and team members and you will achieve any goals you set for your organization; you will likely achieve them faster than you ever thought possible.

It took me over a decade to build out these tools, to refine them, to fully implement them throughout the DLP organizations. If it takes you a year or two or three to get this system fully implemented in your business, you're still way ahead of the game.

Everything you need to get started—implementation guides, training videos, and templates—are available to you and your team at DLPElite.com. In addition, you can subscribe to the *Building an Elite Organization* podcast for a step-by-step overview of the Elite Execution System. Also, be sure to register for our live or virtual events and webinars to help you succeed with the Elite Execution System as you continue on this journey for many years to come.

Building an Elite Organization is an amazing ride. Have fun with it as you and your team keeping marching that 20-Mile March on your path to greatness.

ACKNOWLEDGMENTS

I would first and foremost like to thank the Lord my Savior for all He has done for me, and the incredible opportunity He has provided to me to serve Him and to show love and use my God-given abilities to achieve God-sized goals that please Him.

I would like to thank my wife, Carla, who has been by my side showing me support, love, and patience over the past ten years. Being married to the CEO of a high-growth business is no easy task.

I would also like to acknowledge Jim Collins, Gino Wickman, Verne Harnish, John Maxwell, Sean Covey, Hal Elrod, and Mark Batterson, the great thought leaders who have not only guided my growth but have also been instrumental in the development of the Elite Execution System.

I would like to acknowledge the amazing elite world-class leaders and team members at DLP who have helped develop, test, and improve the Elite Execution System and the tools we have used over the past decade-plus. I appreciate your patience and willingness to support all of the new and consistently evolving set of tools, some of which have turned out to be staples of the Elite Execution System and others that turned out to not work at all.

Finally, I would like to acknowledge the passionate, gritty, driven, positive, relentless, and humble entrepreneurs and business scalers who are never satisfied with the status quo, who want to constantly improve themselves and their businesses so that they can create a bigger impact on the world, in their communities, and for their clients. These elite producers have the discipline, energy, and passion to never give up and never give in. You inspire and motivate me to continue to seek to serve and to give all I can. Thank you.

ABOUT THE AUTHOR

DON WENNER is the Founder and CEO of DLP Capital, a leading private real estate investment and financial services company. DLP has been ranked as an *Inc.* 5,000 Fastest-Growing US company for nine consecutive years, with an average three-year growth rate exceeding 400 percent and more than $1.5 billion in assets. Named one of the top fifteen real estate professionals by REAL Trends and *The Wall Street Journal* for eight years straight, Don has closed more than $5 billion in real estate transactions. He resides in St. Augustine, Florida, with his wife and two sons.

CPSIA information can be obtained
at www.ICGtesting.com
Printed in the USA
BVHW080207191021
619151BV00003B/6

9 781544 517490